THE CONQUEST

OF

ILLUSION

THE author has something to say, which he perceives
to be true and useful, or helpfully beautiful. So far
as he knows, no one has yet said it ; so far as he knows,
no one else can say it. He is bound to say it, clearly
and melodiously if he may ; clearly, at all events. In
the sum of his life he finds this to be the thing, or
group of things, manifest to him—this, the piece of
true knowledge, or sight, which his share of sunshine
and earth has permitted him to seize. He would fain
set it down for ever ; engrave it on the rock, if he
could ; saying, ' This is the best of me ; for the rest,
I ate, and drank, and slept, loved, and hated, like
another ; my life was as the vapour, and is not ; but
this I saw and knew : this, if anything of mine, is
worth your memory.'

RUSKIN, *Sesame and Lilies.*

THE CONQUEST

OF

ILLUSION

by

J. J. VAN DER LEEUW

LL.D.

A QUEST BOOK
Published under a grant from The Kern Foundation

THE THEOSOPHICAL PUBLISHING HOUSE
Wheaton, Ill., U.S.A.

Madras, India / London, England

Printed in the United States of America.

Original edition 1928.

Quest Book paperback edition 1966.

This edition published by special arrangement with
Alfred A. Knopf Inc. (New York) and
George Allen & Unwin Ltd. (London).

Printed in the United States of America.

1525005
TABLE OF MATTER

THIS BOOK IS DEDICATED TO

J. KRISHNAMURTI

AND TO THE MEMORY OF HIS BROTHER

NITYĀNANDA

IN TOKEN OF AN UNVARYING FRIENDSHIP
AND IN REMEMBRANCE OF
OJAI DAYS

CHAPTER ONE

THE QUEST OF LIFE

*For this feeling of wonder shows that you are a philosopher, since
wonder is the only beginning of philosophy.*—PLATO, *Theaetetus.*

THE PHILOSOPHY OF EXPERIENCE

IT is one of the platitudes of our age to say that the time for
words is past and the time for action has come. All around
us is this clamour for action, all around the contempt for mere
words, however verbose the exponents of the action cult may
be. But then, even action needs expounding.

Yet there is sound reason underlying this impatience with
words that are not vitally connected with action. Especially
in philosophy we have suffered for many years from a deluge
of words, barren of action, and consequently the man in the
street has come to look upon philosophy as a pretentious
speculation leading nowhere, an intellectual game, subtle and
clever, sometimes not even that, but always without practical
value for the life of everyday. Often it has been such ;
disguising its lack of reality under the cloak of a difficult and
technical terminology it frightened away the investigating
layman and made him feel that it was his fault, his short-
coming which prevented him from understanding its profound mysteries. Only the bold and persevering investigator
discovers that its cloak often hides but a pitiful emptiness.

The profoundest minds have ever spoken the simplest
language. The thought of Plato may be deep, his language

is ever simple and may be understood by any cultured man. Here Oriental philosophy may well teach the West. Lao Tze, Patanjali, Gautama speak a language of utter simplicity, by the side of which Kant or Hegel appears ponderous and confused. When a thing is clear to a philosopher he must be able to say it in simple and intelligible language. If he fails to do so and if many volumes must needs be written to expound what he might have meant, it is a certain sign that his knowledge was confused. Only imperfect knowledge goes hidden under a load of words.

But apart from its intricate and unbeautiful language philosophy has often been a stranger to life. See again how the truly great touch life at every step and ever bring into this world of daily life the fire which they steal from the gods. If our philosophy leads to wisdom and not merely to know-ledge it must bear fruit in action. Hear Epictetus the Stoic :

> The first and most essential part of philosophy is that con-cerning the application of rules, such as for instance : not to lie. The second part is that concerning proofs such, as for instance : whence does it follow that one should not lie ? The third part is the confirmation and analysis of the first two parts, for instance : how does it follow that this is a proof ? For what is a proof ? What is a consequence, what a contra-diction ? What truth, what error ? Hence the third part is necessary because of the second and the second because of the first ; but the most necessary and that in which we must find peace, is the first. We, however, do the opposite ; for we stop at the third part and all our interest concerns it ; but the first we neglect entirely. Hence we do lie, but we know by heart the proof that we should not lie. (*Encheiridion*, 52.)

It is in the acid test of daily life that the worth of a philo-sophy is proved. Morality is never the beginning, but always the end. While knowledge may remain a stranger to action, wisdom, being experience of life, can never fail to stamp our every word and action with its seal.

Morality, however, or ethics, is but one way in which wisdom becomes action ; true philosophy inspires civilization at every point. There was never a Platonist worthy of the name who did not leave the world the better for his philosophy, whether he was poet or politician. But it is only when philosophy has ceased to be merely intellectual and has become experience of living truth that it can be thus creative.

It is possible, with infallible logic, to build up an intellectual structure that has the appearance of a philosophy of life, but is in reality a phantasm of death. Only when philosophy as experience is rooted in our consciousness, and thence draws the life-giving force that makes of it a living organism, can it bear fruits that nourish man. Thus the facts on which a vital philosophy is based must needs be of a psychological nature or, using a much dreaded word, 'subjective.' But then, even though we may be happily oblivious of it, all facts are of a psychological nature, since we do not know a thing except in so far as it becomes awareness in our consciousness. The division of knowledge or truth into subjective and objective is misleading ; the moment a thing becomes knowledge it is subjective, though its validity may well be objective. A fact of our consciousness or psychological truth may well be of objective value in so far as it is not a merely personal appreciation, but of universal application. In that case the method is subjective, the value objective. On the other hand there are facts which we call objective since they belong to what we call the outer world, but which are subjective in value since they apply to us only. It is the confusion of the two ways in which the word subjective is used, the one pertaining to *method*, when subjective means 'belonging to the consciousness,' and the other pertaining to *validity*, when subjective means ' of personal value only,' which makes us dread the term subjective. There are many facts of the consciousness which we come to know in a subjective way, but which yet are objective in validity since they hold good not only for us, but for all men.

It is therefore no disparagement of philosophy to say of it that, in contrast with science, its method is subjective. Did we but realize it, there is greater safety in the knowledge of our own consciousness, which is direct, than in the knowledge of the world around us, which is indirect.

In this book the philosophical method will be psychological and based on experience of consciousness rather than argumentative and based on logical proof. I do not hesitate to use the central reality of mystical experience, namely the experience of what Bucke calls ' cosmic consciousness,' as a fact of the uttermost consequence in philosophy. The imposing testimony of all ages, which Bucke has gathered in his well-known book, goes far to prove the universal validity of an experience which some would discredit as ' merely subjective.' It is subjective in so far as we approach it through our own consciousness, it is more than subjective, since in cosmic consciousness we share a Reality of which we are but an infinitesimal part. The race is growing towards this cosmic consciousness which is but the concluding chapter in an evolution of consciousness, leading from unconscious-ness through self-consciousness to cosmic consciousness. It is in this mystical experience that the intellect is transcended and knowing becomes being. Far from being the vague emotionalism or the hysterical transports which at times have usurped the name of mysticism, true mystical experience is a most definite reality. A philosophy based on it is no longer a philosophy of reasoning only, but primarily a philosophy of experience, reasonably expounded.

It is here that philosophy can break through that ring-pass-not which Kant drew round the thing in itself, proclaiming it unknowable by reason. No doubt he was right, but this does not mean that the thing in itself cannot ever be known in any way. In a later chapter it will be shown how the experience of the thing in itself in the world of the Real is a possibility and how through that experience philosophy can be liberated from the Kantian doom. In this liberation the faculty of the intuition, or knowledge by experience, is consciously used and with this a new world opens for philosophy, in fact, a new philosophy is born. No longer is philosophy then a matter of intellectual belief, a result of irrefutable argument and convincing proof ; it has become the experience of living man, life of his life, being of his being, the experience of truth.

THE BIRTH OF WONDER

There is no more pathetic spectacle than that of an age which is bored with life. Materially our modern world is richer than perhaps any preceding age ; spiritually we are paupers. Not all our truly wonderful physical accomplishments, not all our abundance of amusements and sensations can hide the fact that we are poor within. In fact, the task of the latter is but to hide the poverty within ; when our inner life is arid we must needs create artificial stimuli from without to provide a substitute, or at least cause such an unbroken succession of ever varying sensations that we have no time to notice the absence of life from within.

There are but few who can bear either solitude or silence, and find a wealth of life arising in themselves even when there is naught from without to stimulate. Yet such alone are happy, such alone truly live ; where we find the craving for amusement and sensation from without we see an abject confession of inner lifelessness. There lies the difference between the quick and the dead, some are dead even in life, others can never die since they are life. We all seek life, since life is happiness and life is reality. But it is only when we have the courage to cease from sensationalism and outer stimulants that we may be successful in our quest.

Philosophy is the quest of life. It is more than a love of wisdom, unless we understand wisdom as being different from knowledge, as different as life is from death. Wisdom is knowledge which is experience and therefore life ; the quest of wisdom is in reality the quest of life. It is true that the name of philosophy has often been used to cover a game of intellectual question and answer which leaves men no richer than before. Thus the average man distrusts philosophy and accuses it of giving stones for bread. But real philosophy is not the intellectual solving of problems ; in the words of Plato, philosophy is the birth of wonder, and he is the true philosopher who begins to wonder about life, not he who is certain of having solved that which is beyond solution. It is profoundly true that, until we can see the wonder of life all around us, unless we see ourselves surrounded by a mystery that challenges our daring exploration, we have not entered on the path of philosophy.

Unawakened man knows only facts, no mysteries, to him things are their own explanation ; the world is there and what else is there to know ? Such is the animal outlook ; to the bovine mind pastures may be good or bad, but they need no explanation. Thus unawakened man is content with the facts of existence—his environment, his food, his work, his family and friends are so many facts surrounding him, pleasant or unpleasant, but never in need of explanation. To speak to him of a mystery hidden in his life and his world would not convey any meaning ; he exists and the fact of his existence is sufficient unto him. Death and life themselves may for a while cause him anxiety or joy, but even then they do not arouse any questions ; they are familiar and customary. It is the very familiarity of life which hides its mystery to the animal mind. That which seen once would be a marvel becomes familiar when seen a hundred times and ceases to suggest the possibility of further explanation ; have we not switched on the electric light so many times that the unexplained wonder of electricity is lost in the familiarity of the action and the fact has become its own explanation ?

There was a time, in the childhood of humanity, when primitive man lived in a world of mystery, moving among dark fears and unknown terrors. But even then, though the mystery was felt and the world was seen as in a dream, the possibility of questioning the mystery did not suggest itself—primitive man was too much part of nature to question and investigate. With the dawn of intellect the mystery of primitive man is lost and naught but facts in their vulgarity remain ; in the sublime ignorance of a self-satisfaction, which doubts neither itself nor the world, man moves among mysteries which, could he but realize them, would strike terror into his heart. And should he occasionally catch a glimpse of the mystery of life he but hastens to cover it up and even deny it, lest the comfort of his intellectual slumber should be disturbed. Rather than risk the chance of an upheaval of the familiar and comfortable facts of his existence he will shut his eyes to the unexplained and burn at the stake those who persist in seeing and questioning.

The time, however, comes for most of us, when catastrophe and suffering shock us out of the ruts of familiarity, when our old world is destroyed beyond hope of recovery. It is as if the universe, in which, but a few days before, we moved about with the easy certainty of unawakened man, had disappeared overnight and each familiar object and event has become a dark and terrible mystery. Thus would the traveller feel who, waking from a dreamless slumber, finds that he has slept by the side of a deadly reptile, unaware of its proximity and happy in his ignorance.

The awakening to the mystery of life is a revolutionary event ; in it an old world is destroyed so that a new and better one may take its place, and all things are affected by the change. We ourselves have become mysterious strangers in our own eyes and tremblingly we ask ourselves who we are, whence we came, whither we are bound. Are we the being who is called by our name, whom we thought we knew so well in the past ? Are we the form we see in the mirror, our body, offspring of our parents ? Who, then, is it that feels and thinks within us, that wills and struggles, plans and dreams, that can oppose and control this physical body which we thought to be ourselves ? We wake up to realize that we have never known ourselves, that we have lived as in a blind dream of ceaseless activity in which there was never a moment of self recollection.

Our very consciousness is *terra incognita ;* we know not the working of our own mind. What is it that happens when we think or feel, when a moral struggle takes place in us, when we are inspired, respond to beauty or sacrifice ourselves for others ? It is as if we were prisoners in the vast palace of our consciousness, living confined to a small and bare room beyond which stretch the many apartments of our inner world, into which we never penetrate, but out of which mysterious visitors—feelings, thoughts, ideas and suggestions, desires and passions— come and pass through our prison, without our knowing whence they come or whither they go. In our consciousness we knew but results, we saw but that which rose to the surface and became visible ; now we begin to realize a vast and unexplored world of mystery which, *mirabile dictu,* is the world of our own inner life.   We are discovering the wonder of life.

It is everywhere around us, this wonder of life, nothing now is common or familiar, everything throbs with a mysterious life which is there for us to explore.   The sacred enthusiasm of the investigator claims us, we desire to know as a starving man desires food, we cannot live unless we know ; we will know if it must cost our lives.   Thus are we born as philosophers.

THE MYSTERY OF LIFE

The mystery of life is not a problem to be solved ; it is a reality to be experienced.   Beware of the man who claims to have solved the problem of life, who would explain its complexities and, with deadly logic, build a system in which all the facts of our existence may be pigeon-holed and neatly stored away.   He stands condemned by his own claim.   The child which sees wonder in all the world around it, to whom the shells with which it plays on the beach are objects of breathless excitement and thrilled amazement, is nearer to divine truth than the intellectualist who would strip a world of its mystery and takes pride in showing us its anatomy in ruthless dissection.   For a while it may satisfy evolving man to know that the splendours of a sunset are but the breaking of light-rays in a moist atmosphere ; he will come to realize that he may have explained the method, but has not touched the mystery at all.   Recovering from the sureness of youth, never doubting itself, awakened man returns to the wonder of childhood and once again sees a world which, as the years pass by, deepens in mystery and beauty, but is never exhausted or explained.

Many are the systems claiming to explain life, contradictory in their premises and consequently in their conclusions. They may be clever, they may fit perfectly in all their details, but life itself never evades them; were it possible to contain life in a system it would no longer be life, but death. Life is ever changing, ever becoming, yet eternal in its abiding reality and the desire to grasp and hold it, to see it stretched out before us, as a butterfly in its glass case is destined ever to be disappointed. Our systems of theology and philosophy, yes, even science, are but as momentary glimpses of a rapid movement; they may show us an instant of that movement in frozen immobility, the movement itself can never be contained in them. And yet, even though the attempt to solve the problem of life and explain it logically is doomed to failure, still the yearning to understand more, to know our own meaning and purpose is so irresistible that even the thought of failure cannot hold it back.

The thirst for truth is a sacred aspiration; like water seeking to gain its true level its onward pressure is unending until its purpose is fulfilled, its object achieved. Such a fundamental desire cannot exist only to be frustrated; the very existence of the desire for truth is the promise of its fulfilment and prophesies achievement. Fundamental instincts are never wholly mistaken; if truth were not for man the desire for truth would not be as a burning unrest in his heart, the eagle ever eating out Prometheus' liver which ever grows again. That man should desire truth above all things is right, that he should be willing to sacrifice himself, his years, yes, his very life, to achieve does but show the nobility of the desire. But when, in blindness of materialism, he wants to *have* truth, to grasp and hold her, to lock her between the pages of a book, to make an object, a thing of that which is the heart of things, then the nobility of his aspiration is lost and the hero of yesterday becomes an object of pity, at whom the great gods smile in compassion.

Though ever again men may claim to have found truth and to possess her, truth herself remains untouched ; truth is the mystery of life which the hand of man can never reach. Truth never descends to our world of error, he who would know must ascend towards that world of Reality where he can see face to face and, for a while, becomes living truth. But it is ever man who must climb the mountain of reality, the Vision on the Mount does not descend into the valley. Thus it is possible for man to know the mystery of life ; solve it he never can, still less contain it in an intellectual system, however logical. Life is not logical, though logic is the alphabet which we must learn if we would speak the language of life, which is truth. And yet no intelligible language can tell of the vision to him who has not seen it ; each must tread the weary path up the mountain-side by himself and reach the bare and lonely top where alone the vision can be seen. We may point out the path, tell of the hardships on the way, the dangers to be avoided and the obstacles to over-come, but none may tell the final mystery—its name is Experience.

The mystery of life is not a problem to be solved, it is a reality to be experienced.

THE VISION ON THE MOUNT

Once we begin to question the world, to demand an answer from our daily existence, we embark on a long and perilous voyage of exploration. Not too lightly should we leave these familiar shores ; unless we are willing to suffer hardship, to toil and persevere when all seems lost, to sail on towards the unknown even though death may be our share, we had better stay at home and hug the shores we know. Yet, if we dare and persevere what glories open up before us, what undreamed joys become ours ! All achievement is to be paid in toil and hardship ; that which comes easily and is given to us, is never the treasure that is lasting.

He who would leave the valley of familiar life in order to climb the far off mountain has to buy his achievement with unknown dangers and continual hardship. His friends will mock at him when he leaves the village of his youth, the place of sunshine and familiar sights, the home and fireside where he is safe from the dangers of the world. Why should he leave all that makes life dear and risk it in futile endeavour after the impossible ? But he in whom the yearning has been born does not heed the mockery ; there is that within him which will not let him rest until he has achieved. And yet, when once he has left the haunts of man and has entered the dense and tangled woods that cover the foothills, he may well doubt whether he has done right. Here is no path to guide him, no sunshine to give him his bearings ; the dense vegetation around seems to shut out the very world and for weary days he hews his way through the tangled growth.

Gradually he ascends and reaches the higher slopes where new and more terrible dangers await him—barren rocks and deadly precipices, cold and piercing winds, treacherous snowfields to be traversed with chasms hidden beneath their smooth surface. His very footsteps dislodge the snow and avalanches threaten with sudden death, yet he climbs on, frost and starvation have no terrors for him, for far ahead shows the mountain top which he must reach. Many a time would he give up his struggle and succumb to the weariness that envelops him, but ever again the voice from within urges him on, the voice that promises achievement.

Then come the last and fearful hours when his lungs can hardly breathe the rarefied air and progress becomes ever slower and more painful. His hands bleed where the sharp rock has torn their flesh, his every step is a burden, in agony he climbs the final slope and reaches the top, where he sinks down, panting and exhausted.

But when he lifts his head and looks around, a new world meets his eye. Far below he sees the woods where he struggled in darkness, lost and erring, beyond again he sees the village of his youth, further yet other villages and cities. But he himself is now lord of all, he has forsaken his world to find a greater World, renounced the familiar sights of life to find the Vision of the mountain top. Forgotten now his hardships, forgotten the long and painful struggle ; in the light of this new world he knows but the bliss which the Vision brings to those who gain it. Henceforth this is his world, the world of the mountain top, henceforth this is his inspiration, the Vision on the Mount. He who has seen it can never again be the same man, he has seen the world stretched out at his feet, has known himself the conqueror of life and death and, wherever he goes, his eyes behold that Vision.

When he descends again and returns from the heights to the valleys in which men live he comes with a new joy singing in his heart and with a solitude which henceforth will make him lonely even in the crowded city. For he moves amongst men who know not the Vision of the mountain top, men whose sight does not reach further than their neighbour's street, and how can he speak to them of the unutterable things which he beheld in the solitude and splendour of the mountain top ? Those who knew him see that he has come back a changed man, that, like the Ancient Mariner, he has a look in his eyes which makes men feel less certain of themselves and causes them to pause for a while in their hurried stride. And he, in whatsoever place he finds himself, ever sees the Vision before him, he sees it even in the ugliness and misery of the lives of men, he hears the Song of Joy singing even through their cries of pain, whatever he beholds is illumined by the glory he has seen.

The familiar sights of his youth have now gained a new and sometimes terrible meaning. Nothing can be commonplace or meaningless to him who has seen the Vision on the Mount. The mystery of life is as a secret Voice within, telling of new and wonderful meanings in all that surrounds him. To some he speaks of the Vision he has seen, of the terrible path he has trodden, and possibly they too feel the yearning for the mountain top and leave life in order to find it again in fuller measure. But though he may tell of his experience, tell of the vision he has seen, each man to whom he speaks must in solitude make the ' flight of the alone to the Alone ' and gain the Vision of which no words can ever tell.

Truly, not lightly should we question and explore the world with which we are familiar, which we seem to know so well, for once we have begun this voyage of exploration there is no turning back to the state of content which knew not doubt or question. It is a great but terrible thing when doubt is born, terrible in that it destroys the old world, great in that it opens the way to a new and nobler one.

CHAPTER TWO

FROM THE UNREAL TO THE REAL

Woe! Woe!
Thou hast destroyed it!
The beautiful world!
Woe! Woe!
Thou hast destroyed! Destroyed!

Create! Create!
Build it again
In thy heart,
The beautiful world!
Create! Create! Create!

GOETHE, *Faust I.*

OUR DUAL UNIVERSE

IT is in the most familiar things of life that the deepest mystery lies hidden. If there is anything about which we feel sure, with which we think ourselves fully and entirely familiar, it is this world surrounding us, the world of our daily life. Around us we are aware of this world, solid and visible, a world so real to us that it would seem madness to doubt its reality. We can see and feel that world, lift the heavy and solid objects in it, hurt ourselves against their unyielding immobility and are impressed all the time by this fundamental fact of our existence—that there, opposite us, independent and apart from us, stands a physical world, utterly and entirely real, solid and tangible.

Within ourselves we are aware of another world, equally real to us, equally accepted as a basic fact of our existence.

But it is a world of consciousness, of life, of awareness, a world which we associate with the feeling that we are ' we '. As a rule, however, our attention is not directed towards that world within, and for most of us it remains a vague and mysterious realm, out of which thoughts and feelings, desires and impulses, flashes of inspiration and sudden ideas seem to emerge, entering into our daily existence with a compelling power that will not be denied. These strange inner happenings also we accept as facts, knowing even less about them than about the solid world of ' material realities ', in which we are so immersed and engrossed. We are thus faced by this strange fact—that the world of our own consciousness is unfamiliar to us, even though it is our very self, and that the world outside, which we assume to be not self, seems quite familiar and well known.

Such then is the fundamental structure of our daily life—a solid, tangible, material world without and a mysterious realm of consciousness within, forming a duality which most of us never come to doubt. In this primitive dualism we live our lives and we look upon our perceptions and our actions as an interplay between those worlds—sensations coming to us from the world outside and forming perceptions in our consciousness, from which again volition and action go forth to change and influence that outer world.

This sense of duality, of an outer and an inner world, is so familiar to us, enters so much into every moment of our lives, that, whenever questions arise with regard to the problems of life, we always, in those questions, assume and presuppose this primitive duality as a fact which needs no proving, *without even being aware that we introduce it*. We unconsciously base our reasoning, yes, the very methods of our analysis and logic, on this fundamental duality which we accept because we have never thought about it. In the quest of truth, however, we must be utterly free from prejudice and ruthlessly sincere, never accepting a fact, cherished though it may be and hallowed by universal recognition, without first challenging its reality, even though such a challenge might appear superfluous. Only thus can we prevent error from entering into our very questions.

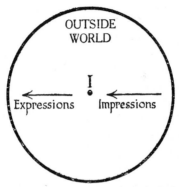

DIAGRAM ONE.—Interaction between the world and myself.

Let us then consider the two elements of our universe, the world of consciousness within and the world of appearances without, and see how we come to know of them. With regard to the consciousness or life side of our twofold universe there can be no doubt ; the fact that we are, something and somehow, is the basis of all our knowledge, of all our awareness. ' Cogito, ergo sum ' is still the starting point of all investigations, the very words ' I think ' already imply the basic fact, ' I am '.

In ordinary consciousness all I know is an unceasing, everflowing modification of my inner life, of my very being ; my awareness, or state of consciousness, is different at every moment. I know nothing but these states of consciousness or awareness ; nothing, idea or object, exists for me unless

I am aware of it, that is to say, unless it is awareness in my consciousness.

It is difficult to realize this simple fact that, when we say we know a thing, whether as a sense perception or as an idea, all we do really know is a state of consciousness corresponding in some way to the object or to the idea. We live and move and have our being in the world of our consciousness and it is the only world we know directly, all else we know through it. This means that all knowledge except that of our own consciousness is derived knowledge; we experience an awareness in our consciousness and thence derive the existence of something that has produced the awareness.

Hence our relation to the appearance side of our universe, the outer world, is very different from our relation to the consciousness side of it ; the last we know directly, it is our very being, the other we know only indirectly, in so far as our being is modified by it in what we call ' awareness '. Therefore, while we cannot doubt the fact that we are aware of things and that we are experiencing modifications of consciousness, we must carefully scrutinize our conclusions about an objective universe around us which produces the perceptions in our consciousness. The latter are indubitable, the former but a conclusion which we rightly or wrongly derive from them. Yet, curiously enough, we feel perfectly confident about the objective universe around us, even though it is a derived knowledge, and feel somewhat uncertain as to the world of consciousness within ; the stone at our feet is ever more real to us than our consciousness within. Yet we only know that stone in and through our consciousness.

THE WAY OF SENSE-PERCEPTION

Yet we feel convinced of the objective reality of the world surrounding us, ' just as we see it,' in fact, we forget all about our consciousness as intermediary between ourselves and the object and look upon the awareness in our consciousness as identical with the object itself. Thus, when we see a green tree, we do not doubt for a moment that the tree stands there, a hundred yards away from us, exactly as we see it, and we have gone a long way in philosophical realization when we can *realize* and not merely believe that the tree which we see is but the image produced in our consciousness by the tree which *is* and that the two are by no means identical.

The primitive and unthinking way of explaining sense-perception implies that, through the senses, a faithful image of the world around us is reproduced in our consciousness in such a way that image and reality are exactly alike (see Plate I). In order to explain this process still further we compare it to the action of a photographic camera, where through the lens an entirely accurate and faithful picture is reproduced on the sensitive plate. Satisfied with that explanation we sink back into our unquestioning acceptance of the world around us, glad that everything is so simple and never suspecting that we have not explained anything at all. How the image reaches our consciousness through the darkness of the sensory nerves and the brain matter is a question which does not even occur in the primitive explanation. And yet, even if the senses produced a faithful image of the world surrounding us, that image again would have to be perceived by the consciousness and with regard to the perception of that image we should find ourselves faced by exactly the same difficulty as with regard to the perception of the outer world itself. We have merely shifted the problem one step, and, to the unthinking mind, such a shifting or re-statement of a problem is generally quite acceptable by way of explanation.

However, the image which the senses give us of the world around can never be a faithful one ; our senses are selective

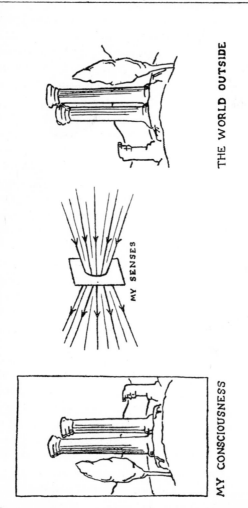

THE WORLD OUTSIDE

MY SENSES

MY CONSCIOUSNESS

PLATE ONE :—PRIMITIVE IDEA OF SENSE PERCEPTION
The image in my consciousness a replica of the objects outside.

and can only interpret those elements of the world around us to which they are able to respond. Thus, in the case of sound and light, we need only look at a table of vibrations in air and ether to realize how extremely small the groups of vibrations are to which eye and ear react. With regard to all the other vibrations we are practically insensitive, we only know them by inference.

It is a very useful exercise to think ourselves into a state of consciousness, where those elements of the world around us, to which our senses respond now, would be non-existent and the contents of our world-image would be furnished by elements to which our present senses do not respond. Imagine two beings meeting and comparing their knowledge of the world, a human being with our five senses and an imaginary being with the senses we lack. Each of them would be aware of a world around him, each of them, unless they were philosophers, would be quite certain that he perceived the world exactly as it was there, outside, and that he perceived all there was to be perceived of it. Yet their two worlds would be utterly unlike; could we for a moment perceive the other being's world there would be nothing in it familiar to us or resembling any feature of our world. And yet, the other being would have as much right to call his world the real world, as we should have to call ours the world as it really is. But from the standpoint of reality no one has a right to call his world *the* world ; it is *his* world and nothing more, his selective interpretation of reality.

With the understanding of this truth our primitive explanation of sense-perception as a faithful reproduction of the world around us collapses, and our world-image, far from being identical with the real world, becomes but our specific interpretation of that world ; our world is but *our* version of *the* world.

It is well to ponder deeply over this very simple fact of the selectivity of our senses and thoroughly familiarize ourselves with the idea that what we see around us is not the world at all, but rather the peculiar interpretation of that world which we as human beings, because of the nature of our five senses, make. It is not sufficient to agree intellectually with this and say that the argument is clear and that we acknowledge it to be true ; philosophy must be realization if it is to be worth anything, and the truth we realize must become part of our very consciousness. Our innate superstition that the world we see is *the* world indeed is so deeply ingrained in our nature that it will rise again and again and make us believe that our world-image is the world in reality. Our primitive illusions need to be rudely shaken before a wider knowledge can be born.

Even if our senses are selective and do but interpret certain features of the world around us we might yet be tempted to say that, in so far as they do interpret that world, they interpret it faithfully and that the colours we see or the sounds we hear are there, around us, exactly as we are aware of them. Even a superficial study of the physiology of sense-perception, however, is sufficient to break down this last stronghold of sense-realism. Since the problem is the same for all our senses we may take the eye, and the sense of vision connected with it, as representative of the principles of sense-perception in general.

The light-vibrations which reach the eye are focussed through the lens and act on the retina behind the eyeball, causing structural and chemical changes in it. If, at this stage of the process of seeing, we, as it were, tapped the wire, we should as yet find no trace of that which later on will become our awareness of the green tree ; all we find are structural and chemical changes in the rods and cones which form the upper layer of the retina. It is of the utmost importance to realize that the knowledge, so far conveyed to the body from the outer world, is contained in these chemical and structural changes, which in turn affect the optic nerve along which a message is conveyed to that area in the brain which corresponds to the sense of vision. Still there is no question of a blue sky or a green tree ; all we can hope to find in the brain, if we tap the wire at this stage of the process, is a change in the particles of the brain matter which are affected by the message conveyed along the optic nerve.

Then suddenly we, the living individual, in our consciousness, are aware of the green tree or, as we express it, we ' see ' the green tree. (See Plate II.) This last stage is the great mystery of sense-perception, and neither physiology nor psychology has yet bridged for us that gap between the last perceptible change in the brain and our awareness of the object with its colours and shapes.

Even in the final stage of the physiological process, which is the change in the brain matter, there is no question whatsoever of colour, shape or form, there are only structural and chemical changes in the optical apparatus. It is only when we, the living creature, interpret in our own consciousness that final stage that there is the green tree, the whole world of light and colour around us. *But there is no green tree until we reach that consciousness stage ;* there is, no doubt, some unknown reality which reacts on our senses and somehow produces in our consciousness the awareness of the green tree and will produce that awareness each time it reacts on our consciousness, but there is nothing to show that this unknown reality in any way looks like a green tree. For all we know it may be a mathematical point, having within itself certain properties which, reacting on a human consciousness, produce there the different qualities which make up the image of the green tree as we see it. We, however, substitute the image produced in our consciousness for the unknown reality without and make believe that we are perceiving that selfsame green tree which is the image produced in our consciousness, that is to say, we think we are *perceiving* as an objective reality that which we are *projecting* as an image in the world of our consciousness. This substitution is pictured in Plate II, which shows the different stages of the process of vision, the unbridged gap between brain and consciousness, the arising of the image of the green tree in the consciousness and the projection of that image in lieu of the unknown reality. We, as it were, clothe the nakedness of the unknown reality with the image produced in our consciousness.

The same facts, which are true for the sense of vision, hold good for our perception through any of the senses ; thus there is no question of sound but in our consciousness, no question of taste or smell but in our consciousness, no question of hardness or softness, of heaviness or lightness but in our consciousness ; our entire world-image is an image arising in our consciousness because of the action on that consciousness by some unknown reality.

OUR BODY TOO PART OF OUR WORLD-IMAGE

It is clear from a study of the physiology of sense-perception that all we know of the realities without, or of things in themselves, are the images produced by them in the world of our consciousness. But, curiously enough, even where we find this recognized and understood, we often find the physical body itself and the vibrations reaching it from the unknown objects outside, treated as if they were *not* images in our consciousness, but as if concerning them we knew everything. But how do we know of the existence of any

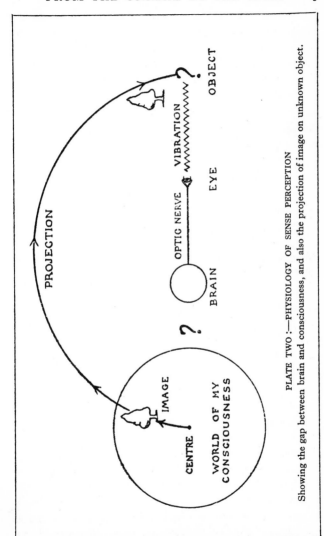

PLATE TWO :—PHYSIOLOGY OF SENSE PERCEPTION

Showing the gap between brain and consciousness, and also the projection of image on unknown object.

vibration ? By sense-perception, aided by scientific instruments which help us to see either the vibration itself or the effect produced by that vibration, showing us its nature. But surely this again is sense-perception and our perception of the vibration which reaches the eye, of the eye itself, the retina and the changes produced in it, of the optic nerve, and of the brain itself, takes place in exactly the same way as our perception of any object belonging to this mysterious outer world. They too : vibration, eye, retina, nerve and brain belong to that world of unknown quantities which in us produces images. Whether the image is that of a green tree an optic nerve, or the grey matter in the brain does not matter, the relation of image to unknown reality is the same for all. The eye, the optic nerve, the brain, and our physical body in general should not be singled out from this world surrounding us ; they one and all belong to the world of unknown reality without, which produces in our consciousness that image which we call the world, but which is only our world-image.

It is the peculiar relation in which we stand to our own body, the intimate link we have with it and which we do not have with regard to any other object in the outer world, which makes us feel that we know all about its reality, even though other things may be full of mystery. We have an inside feeling of our body which we do not have with regard to a stone or a tree, our body appears to us as part of ourselves and we forget that it is as much part of that outer world as the tree or the stone, and that our perception of it as a visible and tangible object takes place in just the same way as our perception of the tree or of the stone. Even the inner feeling we have of our body is but a variety of sense-perception which exists for our body alone. It too is but an awareness produced in our consciousness by an unknown reality, and with regard

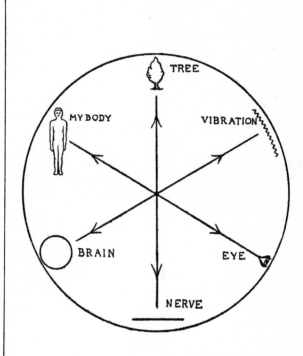

PLATE THREE :—THE WORLD OF MY CONSCIOUSNESS
My body and its organs, too, images in my consciousness.

to it the same mystery exists as with regard to our perception of any other object in the outer world.

This means that we must somewhat revise our conception of the process of sense-perception as pictured in Plate II. In it the object outside was supposed to be unknown, but the vibration which it sent out, the eye reached by that vibration and the nerve and brain affected in consequence, were all accepted as known and familiar quantities and never doubted as objective realities existing there, exactly as we perceive them. It was this ready assumption of the physical body as an independent reality existing without, which caused the gap between the last change in the brain and the image arising in our consciousness. This gap disappears when we realize that our physical body too, as we know it in its shape and colours, with all its qualities, is also an image produced in our consciousness by an unknown reality. Thus the situation becomes that shown in Plate III, where tree, vibration, eye, retina, optic nerve, brain and physical body in general, are one and all shown as images arising in the world of our consciousness.

OUR WORLD AND THE WORLD

There is never a truth but carries in it the possibility of misconception. Thus it is true that the world which we ' see around us ' is an image arising in our consciousness, with which image we subsequently deal as if it were an objective reality, existing apart from our consciousness. But there have been those who, catching a glimpse of this truth, have drawn the conclusion that therefore nothing but their own consciousness was real and that the world-image arising in their consciousness was in some way their own creation, in fact, that they lived in a world of their own making. This misconception, called *solipsism* (from *solus*, alone and *ipse*,

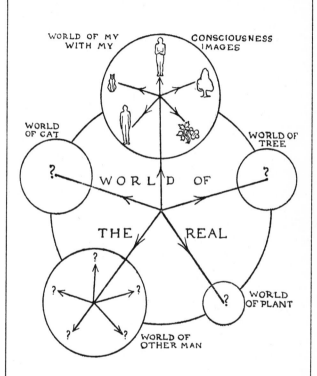

PLATE FOUR :—RELATION OF WORLD OF REALITY
TO CONSCIOUSNESS-WORLDS
Only the images, appearing in my consciousness, are known to me.

self, meaning the outlook which recognizes only my own consciousness as real) is manifestly absurd ; were it true that this world surrounding me is my own spontaneous creation I should be capable of varying that creation at will, and if a tree, or a stone, or any of my fellowmen displeased me I should be able to eliminate them by an effort of the will ceasing in fact to create them. The solipsist is right in saying that what most people conceive to be an objective reality surrounding them is in reality their world-image, but he omits the second and greater truth, namely—that this world-image is produced in our consciousness by the action upon that consciousness of an unknown reality, the real world or world of things in themselves. It is perfectly true that what I take to be an objective world is only the world-image produced in my consciousness, but it is equally true that this world-image is determined in its character by the nature of the things in themselves ; it is my interpretation of them, partial and imperfect, but not containing anything which is not determined, in principle or in essence, by the thing in itself. Every phenomenon in my world-image is intimately and continually connected with a very real thing or event in the world of reality, and the fact that at some moment I might cease to produce a world-image in my consciousness does not for a moment affect conditions in the world of the Real.

The conception of all that surrounds us as image in our consciousness, was represented in Plate III ; we must now go a step further and recognize that there is a world of the Real which, through my consciousness, produces the different images in it. In Plate IV the world of our consciousness with its many images is shown in its relation to *the* world. The smaller circles a* the end of the rays from the centre symbolize the consciousness-worlds of different creatures, more or less limited according to their stage of evolution. In each of these consciousness-worlds a world-image is produced by the action of the things in themselves on that particular consciousness ; each creature only knows its own world-image.

When, therefore, an event takes place in this world of Reality there is produced in the consciousness of each creature concerned an awareness, or image, which is the event as we ' see ' it.

We must not misunderstand this. When I take up a book and drop it on the ground only one event takes place and that is the event as it is in the world of the Real. There is nothing unreal about that event, it is entirely, wholly and thoroughly real. But my awareness of the event, the way in which it presents itself in my world-image is my interpretation of the real event, and that interpretation is only relatively real, real for me, not real in itself. When then, in my world-image, I am aware of my hand grasping the book and dropping it on the ground, what really happens is that in the world of the Real an interaction takes place between that which I am in that world, that which my body and consequently my hand is in that world, and that which the book and the ground are in that world, and that interaction or event is the one and only real event which takes place. What appears in my world-image is my version of it, in which version the unity of the event is broken up in measures of time and space and in a multitude of qualities. Then I externalize my awareness of the event in itself and *that externalized image becomes for me the event itself.* Unreality or illusion never resides in the event, or thing in itself, nor even in my interpretation of it, which is true enough *for me*, but in the fact that I take my interpretation to be the thing in itself, exalting it to the stature of an absolute and independent reality. Referring again to Plate IV we can see how an event, affecting all the

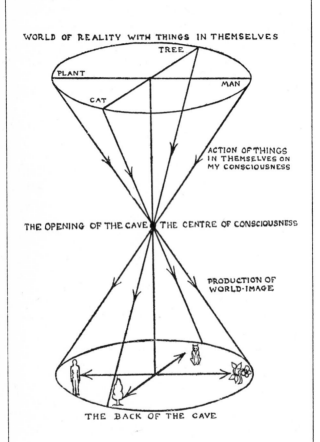

PLATE FIVE :—THE PRODUCTION OF THE WORLD-IMAGE
THROUGH THE CENTRE OF CONSCIOUSNESS
Through the centre is the entrance to the World of Reality.

creatures whose consciousness circles are there represented, would produce a different version or image in the consciousness of each, though the event itself remains one and the same. In fact, though the real world is necessarily the same for all beings, the interpretation of that world must always be different for each.

The relation of the real world to our consciousness and the image produced in it, is again shown in Plate V, but only for one particular consciousness. In it we see how the things in themselves, as they exist in the world of the Real, act on our centre of consciousness and, through it, are projected as images in the world of our consciousness, thus forming our world-image. From this diagram it is clear how, through our consciousness, all things are as it were turned inside out ; *instead of being aware that they act on us from within we gaze upon the image we have produced and wonder how it influences us from without.* It has become our fatal habit thus to look outwards upon the images produced in our consciousness and to forget entirely that they are projected there by the action upon our consciousness of things in the world of the Real. Thus, in our diagram, we are only aware of the lower half, our own world, and, like the prisoners in Plato's cave, we are so used to gaze upon the back wall of our cave and see the shadows moving there, that we forget and even deny the possibility of turning round and knowing the reality which casts the shadows.

It is in his *Republic* that Plato uses this image, in which he compares men to prisoners who live in a cave and are bound in such a way that they can only see the back of the cave, not its opening. Behind them the procession of life moves by, different creatures pass and different events take place. The prisoners cannot see all this, but they do see the shadows cast upon the back of the cave. These shadows are reality to the prisoners, for them they are the world, and, since they have never seen anything else, it does not even occur to them that there can be another world. They may have come to know the different shadows by name and may even have built up a certain knowledge on their observation of the regularly recurring shadows. But all the time, though their knowledge and their observation must necessarily have a certain relation to the reality outside, they deal with shadows and not with real things.

From time to time a prisoner feels the urge to free himself from his bonds and explore the other side of the cave. If he succeeds in doing so he discovers the great secret : that there, outside the mouth of the cave, is a magnificent world of reality, a world of dazzling light and beauty, and that what he used to see on the back wall of the cave were not real things at all, but only shadows. In the beginning his eyes, unused to the light of the real world, would be as blinded ; he would only be aware of light everywhere. But gradually, as he begins to get used to this new world, he learns to distinguish between its creatures and objects, its colours and shapes, and comes to know that world in all its rich variety. Can we not imagine how, inspired by the wonderful discovery he has made, the erstwhile prisoner would go back to those who are still imprisoned in the cave and tell them, full of joy, of the glorious world he has found outside ? But they would only laugh and call him mad ; they know well enough that the only world is the world they see on the back of the cave and that those who would discover other worlds, and call their world a shadow-world, are but dreamers.

Our life is like that of the prisoners in the cave ; we too see only the back of the cave, the wall of our own consciousness on which dance the shadows, the images cast there by the reality which we do not behold. We have come to know the play of these shadows so well that we have been able to build up an entire science concerning them.   This science is right in so far as the shadows have a vital relation to the reality that casts them, but it is ever doomed to find itself confronted by mysteries which in the world of shadows can never be solved, unless some who have seen the real world introduce into these sciences a wider knowledge.   But we are impatient and incredulous when anyone would tell us that the world upon which we gaze is not the world of the Real, but only our world-image.   Yet among us too evidence is not lacking of men, who, throughout the ages, have found freedom from their bondage, who have conquered illusion and discovered that world of Reality of which this world of ours is but a shadow or image, cast in the cave of our consciousness.

ILLUSION AND REALITY

We must, however, be careful about the way in which we characterize this our world as illusion, in fact, the danger of an incomplete statement and subsequent misunderstanding is so great that it hardly seems possible to state the relation as it truly is.

When we say, ' this world around us is unreal, it is illusion,' we make a misleading statement ; when we say, ' this world is real, it is not illusion,' we are even more misleading.   Yet, if we were to think of this world as a strange mixture of real and unreal, that thought would be the most misleading of all.

To begin with, *the* world itself is real, there is nothing unreal whatsoever about a chair or a table, a tree or a stone, about all that which we call the physical world.   It is a common mistake to characterize the physical world as unreal, or less real, and some mental or spiritual world as more real. The physical world *in itself*, the chair and the table *in themselves*, the stone or the tree *in itself*, are one and all as real as

I am myself. But what I usually *call* the table, the chair, the stone or the tree is the image produced in my consciousness by the table, chair, stone or tree as it exists in the world of the Real. These images are only relatively real, that is to say they are real for me, in so far as they are my interpretation of the thing in itself, the shadow cast in my cave. It is when I begin to look upon this image in my consciousness as an outside reality, and identify it with the thing in itself, that illusion enters. Then, in contemplating my image of the thing, I believe myself to be dealing with the thing in itself. *The illusion, therefore, is neither in the thing in itself, nor in the image produced in my consciousness by that thing, but in my conception of the image in my consciousness as the thing in itself ; as an object existing independent of my consciousness.*

This then is the structure and relation of the real world and our world. There is a world of Reality, which world, for the purposes of distinction may have to be subdivided into different ' worlds ' later on. But it is essentially *one* world, the only world, and whatever subdivisions we may find fit to make in it are not marked by labels in that real world, but are marked by our own associations and relative standpoint. That one world is the world as it is, in it things are as they truly are. That world is Life or Truth, or whatever else we may call ultimate Reality ; that world is the Absolute, for there is all that is or was or shall be. In that world there is interaction between the different creatures and objects and as a result of that interaction every creature becomes aware in his consciousness of a world-image, the shadow cast by reality. Since, however, that shadow play is all we normally know of the real world we identify it with that real world and look upon it as a reality independent of our consciousness and standing outside us. That is the great Illusion.

Our world-image is thus the way in which we interpret reality. The many qualities of material objects, their distances and dimensions in space and their change in time, all that belongs to our interpretation, to our image. The tree in the world of the Real is not fifty feet high, its leaves are not green and smooth, its trunk is not rough to the touch and hard and it does not weigh so many hundredweights. All these qualities are my interpretation of the tree in itself and are elements of my world-image. The tree in itself as it exists in the world of the Real may be pictured as a mathematical point, but there is that within it which, each time it reacts upon me, produces in my world-image a certain group of qualities of sound, touch, weight and certain measurements in space together with a certain change or growth in time. It is my particular constitution as a human being which causes me to produce just this type of image ; the same tree in itself no doubt produces a different image in other creatures of whose existence I may not even know.

Because of the fundamental illusion which considers my world-image as an independent reality I come to look upon my image of the tree as if it were the tree itself, I assume space and time and the rich variety of sense-qualities to be independent realities existing there outside me, and I imagine events to be happening within their framework. Having thus objectivated and separated from my consciousness that which is indissolubly part of it I find myself hedged in by problems which no master-mind can ever solve, since they, one and all, are wrong problems, vitiated from the start by illusion. That is why the beginning of philosophy must be a clear understanding and even *experience* of the relation of our world-image to ourselves and to the world of the Real. Unless that is thoroughly clear to us from the beginning and becomes in very truth part of our consciousness we shall find ourselves led astray at each subsequent step. But our philosophy must be more than a mere intellectual understanding, every truth to which we attain must become an experience in our consciousness ; thus alone can philosophy be vital and of real value in human life.

THE EXPERIENCE OF THE WORLD OF THE REAL

If it is true that our world-image is indeed an image produced in the cave of our consciousness by a reality beyond, it is evidently our first task, *to tread, not merely in thought but in reality, the path leading to the world of the Real*. It is here that so many philosophies fall short ; they seem satisfied with having propounded their doctrine and do not feel the necessity of the doctrine becoming reality and experience. Often such philosophical doctrines are but an intellectual structure, strange to life and not the outcome of experience in our own consciousness. Yet such experience should not only be the basis of any philosophical assertion, it should also be the final test of any doctrine.

If once again we look upon Plate V and see how our world-image is projected around us in our consciousness we can see the way we have to go ; we must withdraw ourselves from the enticing images of our own production and turn towards that centre through which the production of our world-image takes place—the depth of our consciousness. That, in the beginning, will be the most difficult part—to abandon for a while our world-image, to relinquish this gay spectacle of time and space and the endless variety of sense-qualities. We must renounce all that, renounce sight and hearing, touch and taste and smell, renounce all that is phenomenon, appearance, image : this entire outer world. But even that is not enough. Our world-image is threefold, there is what we call the physical world, there is the world of our emotions and there is the world of thought.   Most of us have not yet developed waking consciousness or self-consciousness in the world of emotions and in the world of thought, but even so they are as much or as little an outside world as what we term the physical world.   In the simple experiment of thought-transference we can test for ourselves the relative objectivity of a thought-image ; in the imparting of a strong emotion from one person to another, a thing we often experience where masses of people are gathered, we can see that an emotion is not the vague inner thing we often think it to be, but objectively real.   Thus we must not only renounce the physical world with its sense-qualities, but also the crowded worlds of our emotions and thoughts—we must cease for a while to allow any emotion to move us or any thought to modify our consciousness.   Difficult as is the renunciation of our physical world-image, the withdrawing from the worlds of our emotions and thoughts is harder still and requires regular and repeated attempts, stretching sometimes through many years, until success is gained.

Let us then do what so few ever do in our hurried civilization—be alone and be silent.   We should relax all effort, and renounce all sensation coming to us from without, still our emotions and our thoughts and sink back into the depth of our own consciousness, like a diver sinking deep into the cool dark waters.

When thus we sink back into the depth of our own consciousness we come to a state in which nothing seems to be any more, in which we ourselves seem to have lost name and form and all characteristics.   We come to the great Void. It is the ' grey void abysm ' of which Shelley sings in his ' Prometheus Unbound,' in that haunting ' Song of the Spirits ' which leads Asia and Panthea down into the depths of consciousness :

To the deep, to the deep,
    Down, down !
Through the shade of sleep,
Through the cloudy strife
Of Death and of Life ;
Through the veil and the bar
Of things which seem and are,
Even to the steps of the remotest throne,
    Down, down !

Through the grey, void abysm,
    Down, down !
Where the air is no prism,
And the moon and stars are not,
And the cavern crags wear not
The radiance of Heaven,
Nor the gloom to Earth given,
Where there is One pervading, One alone,
    Down, down !

When we reach the Void within, the state in which nothing more seems to be, it would appear as if we were surrounded on all sides by a blank wall and as if it were impossible to proceed any further. Then comes the moment when we must break the habit of ages and, like the prisoner in the cave, dare to turn our faces the other way and find the way out of the cave, find reality, freedom.

We have to move in a dimension we did not know before ; the prisoner in the cave never realized that there was such a thing as a world *behind* him and we can well imagine how, when first he strives towards freedom and ceases to contemplate his shadow-play on the back wall of his cave, nothing seems to remain to him and he too finds himself in the great Void.

The first part of our journey towards reality is the surrendering of our world-image and the turning inwards until we reach the centre of consciousness, the second is to pierce through that centre and find the reality which, acting on that centre produces the world-image in the cave of our consciousness. The experience of going through the centre of consciousness and emerging, as it were, on the other side is very much one of turning inside out. In our ordinary consciousness we are turned outwards towards the world-image which we externalized around us. In going through our consciousness the entire process is reversed, we experience an inversion, or conversion, in which that which was without becomes within. In fact, when we succeed in going through our centre of consciousness and emerge on the other side, we do not so much realize a new world around us as a new world within us. We seem to be on the surface of a sphere having all within ourselves and yet to be at each point of it simultaneously.

It is impossible to describe the world of Reality in the terms of our world-image which is the only language at our command. As Kabir says : ' That which you see is not, and for that which is, you have no words ' (*Tagore*, 49). It is a world of pure Beauty, yet, how express beauty without shape, colour or sound, the ' Beauty unbeheld ' of which Shelley sings ? When we experience it we feel that now we know beauty for the first time and that what we used to call beauty in our world image was but a distorted shadow. But the outstanding reality of our experience in the world of the Real is the amazing fact that nothing is outside us. There is distinction between different beings, the things in themselves, there is multiplicity, there is all that which in our world-image produces the rich variety of outer forms and yet it all is within ourselves ; and when we desire to know we *are* that which we know.

Throughout the ages mystics have attempted to describe their vision of reality and in Bucke's work, *Cosmic Consciousness*, he gives at length the descriptions of the mystic state by those who have experienced it. The evidence is too great to speak of these experiences as being of a ' merely subjective ' value ; they are subjective, as all true experience is, but, like all great experience, they are objective in value and validity.

Plotinus, the father of intellectual mysticism, thus describes the vision of Reality, or the ' Intelligible World ' as he calls it, in *Ennead* v. 8, 4 :

> In this intelligible World everything is transparent. No shadow limits vision. All the essences see each other and interpenetrate each other in the most intimate depth of their nature. Light everywhere meets light. Every being contains within itself the entire Intelligible World, and also beholds it entire in any particular being. All things there are located everywhere, every thing there is all, and all is each thing ; infinite splendour radiates around. Everything is great, for these even the small is great. This world has its sun and its stars ; each star is a sun and all suns are stars. Each of them, while shining with its own due splendour, reflects the light of the others. There abides pure movement ; for He who produces movement, not being foreign to it does not disturb it in its production. Rest is perfect, because it is not mingled with any principle of disturbance. The Beautiful is completely beautiful there, because it does not dwell in that which is not beautiful.

In the mystical experience of the world of reality we use a faculty of knowledge which is only beginning to be born in humanity. It is intuition, knowing by being, realization, the ' Tertium Organum ' of Ouspensky. Without the use of that faculty the world of the Real cannot be known, but we must not say that the things in themselves cannot be known at all. The ring-pass-not, which Kant drew round the thing in itself exists only for those in whom the new faculty or organ of knowledge is not awakened, it is by no means a spell laid on all future humanity, denying to them for ever the possibility of knowing the Real.

One truth emerges from our experience like a mountain

peak from a surrounding plain.   We now realize that *no philosophical problem whatsoever can ever be approached in our world-image*, that there is but one way of approaching these problems which is : to conquer the illusion of our world-image, to enter the world of the Real and, in that Reality, to experience living Truth.

It is only in the Vision from the mountain top that we know reality.   But when we climb the Mount of Reality we must leave behind us all the load of illusion which would weigh us down in our climb and prevent us from ascending.   The burden of our cherished illusions cannot pass through the customs of the real World, we must leave behind all that belongs to our world-image, else we shall not reach the mountain top, we shall not see the Vision.

That Vision alone is life, that Vision is Truth, Beauty, Peace and Joy, having seen it we have entered the world where we truly belong.   When again we return to our daily life and play the game of time and space in our world-image, as we needs must do, we shall yet, through that world-image, ever see the Vision of Reality which we have gained ; through every creature, every object, every event of our world-image a new meaning and a new beauty will shine forth.   Such is the gift of Reality even to our world of illusion.

CHAPTER THREE

INTUITION AND INTELLECT

The principle cause of our uncertainty is that our comprehension of the One comes to us neither by scientific knowledge, nor by thought, as the knowledge of other intelligible things, but by a Presence which is superior to science. When the soul acquires the scientific knowledge of something, she withdraws from unity and ceases being entirely one ; for science implies discursive reason and discursive reason implies manifoldness. To attain Unity we must therefore rise above science, and never withdraw from what is essentially One ; we must therefore renounce science, the objects of science, and every other right except that of the One.

—PLOTINUS, *Ennead* VI., 9, 4.

THE TWOFOLD MIND

ILLUSION is only then part of reality when it is recognized as illusion. It is when we forget the element of relativity in our world-image and exalt the latter to the stature of an independent reality, forgetting subsequently that we have done so, that illusion begins. Then we begin to ask questions which are born of illusion and permeated by it in every fibre, it is then that we begin to abuse the nobility of our minds by applying the intellect to the solution of such pseudo-problems. Then we, and our intellects with us, are bound to our own world-image, become slaves of our own creation, victims of our own error and henceforth our nature is twofold, on the one hand our true being in the world of the Real, functioning freely with unclouded vision, on the other hand our being, externalized in our own world-image, bound to its illusions and doomed to join in the *danse macabre* of our phenomenal world. In that world, our own world-image, our thought is devitalized, our method of knowing a clumsy process in which we study the shadow-play surrounding us and learn to discriminate between its different features. That uninspired and unproductive functioning of the mind in the bondage of our own world-image I call *the intellect*, the free use of the living mind in the world of the Real I call *the intuition*.

The difference between intuition and intellect is the difference between life and death ; the intuition is immediate, certain, creative and progressive, the intellect is barren, sterile, indirect in its methods, uncertain in its conclusions and incapable of seeing truth. In the earlier stages of our evolution our way to knowledge is that of instinct, which is unreasoning and direct in its knowledge. Thus primitive man knows the ways of Nature in a way we cannot rival, thus the animal knows instinctively things which it takes man days or often years to reason out. We need but compare the unerring certainty with which migrating birds find their home, a matter of square feet on the entire surface of our globe, to the clumsy methods which intellectual man needs to find his bearings—maps and compasses, sextants and intricate calculations, the movements of the heavenly bodies and landmarks on the surface of the earth, failing which he is helpless.

With the birth of the intellect instinctive knowledge disappears ; the unconscious unity of life which made the instinct possible is temporarily shut off by the increasing sense of separateness and individuality which makes the birth of the intellect possible. When man no longer hears the voice of instinctive knowledge speaking to him from within, he must needs orientate himself by the laborious method of gathering facts about the world surrounding him and, through analysis and discrimination of these, come to the knowledge of indwelling principles. The way of the intellect is thus a necessary stage, but there is no doubt that man's knowledge in this period lacks creative life. His own world-image holds him in bondage, imprisons the mind in its limitations and illusions. That imprisoned mind, or intellect, is consequently ever subject to the great illusion of the world-image as an objective reality.

Yet there comes a time when the power of illusion weakens and the freed mind once again sees the Vision of the Real. With that the intuition begins to develop as a way of know-ledge, combining in itself the directness of the instinct and the conscious knowledge which the intellect gave. Instinct is an unconscious knowledge ; primitive man knows, but knows not why, cannot express consciously, that which speaks to him from within. In the intuition there is the same flash of direct knowledge, but now the great structure of the intellect has been built up through intervening ages and by its means the intuitive knowledge can descend to our daily life in full consciousness. Without that structure, without the intellect as instrument, the thinker within would not be able to interpret his vision in intelligible language to his fellow-men ; the artist may be ever so great, but he needs an instrument to play on.

It is well to analyze why the indiscriminate use of the intellect in philosophy is so full of dangers. In so far as the intellect is enslaved by the illusion of the world-image as an external reality it does not doubt the objective existence of that world-image as a substantial outside world around us. This means that it accepts all the characteristics of our world-image as objective realities—the qualities of matter, the substantiality of objects, the objective reality of time and space, the diversity and separateness of manifested creatures, all these are elements, the objective reality of which is not doubted as long as the mind is enslaved by illusion. When, subject to illusion, never suspecting even its existence, man begins to ask questions concerning the great problems of life it is inevitable that everyone of these questions is asked from the standpoint of the world-image as external reality, that is to say, every question is permeated by that which we have found to be the fundamental illusion of our daily lives. Hence that illusion not only colours every question we thus ask, but is often the very heart of such a question. This means that, unsuspected by us, there enters into the very fabric of our philosophical questions and problems an element of illusion by which these questions become monstrosities, by which they are vitiated, incapable of solution since they are rooted in error.

All questions, for instance, which have to do with a beginning of time or a beginning of creation, show in the very nature of the problem they touch the unthinking acceptance of time as an objective reality and are consequently problems about which we may think for many years, but which we can never solve. In fact, if we do claim to have solved such a problem we stand condemned by our own claim. It is the same with regard to the unthinking acceptance of spirit and matter, or self and not-self, as a real duality. Endless theories have been advanced to reconcile these two, either by the elimination of one of them or by a kind of compromise in which both are seen as eternally opposite aspects of one great reality. However clever such solutions may be they one and all are doomed to be wrong, since they unquestioningly accept the problem as it is stated without first investigating whether it is not in itself the product of misconception. We might add many such problems and shall in later chapters have ample opportunity to show examples of such wrong questions which yet form the stock problems of philosophy. But at present it is necessary to see why the intellect is insufficient as a philosophical method and approach to truth.

The intellect, as the mind bound to illusion, can but work under the limitations of our world-image. The fundamental structure of that world-image is that of a duality, with myself on the one side and everything else on the other side—self and not-self. The intellect thus necessarily accepts the separateness of all things as a basic fact, accepts the ' otherness ' of the world around me as undeniable and in all its cogitations can never free itself from the burden of that basic structure in which it is imprisoned. It is possible for the intellect to recognize theoretically the existence of unity, unity of life, unity of energy, or what else we may call that which unites all things, but even then separateness and multiplicity impress themselves so very much more forcibly upon the intellect, that the conception of a fundamental unity becomes but a pale shadow by the side of their varied and coloured interplay. The very methods of the intellect —distinguishing between one thing and another, analyzing a thing into its component elements, learning to observe the minutest differences between one case and another—all these point to separateness and multiplicity as the domain of the intellect. For its data the intellect has to rely on sense-perception and deduction from basic principles, out of these it builds its theories and systems.

In so far as science claims but to investigate and explore this outer world surrounding us, the intellect is a sufficient instrument for science, though even in the conclusions of scientific investigations the intuition plays a far greater part than we are apt to credit. Fundamentally, however, sense-perception, analyzed and co-ordinated by the intellect is the method of science and, since science does not concern itself primarily with the fundamental problems of life, there is no objection to be made against the important place the intellect takes in its work.   It is only when we enter the domain of philosophy with its pursuit of ultimate reality that we must recognize the insufficiency of the intellect and consciously use the intuition as a way to knowledge.   For in philosophy we have to do with those very relations of ourselves to the world surrounding us and of this world again to ultimate reality, about which the intellect is so confident, accepting them as they appear to be.   By its acceptance of a dual structure of the world and of multiplicity as the character of this universe the intellect can never do more than see one thing *or* another as true ; it can never see one thing *and* another both as true.   To it the world cannot be one and many at the same time and, even if it might theoretically recognize such a possibility, it cannot realize it as a fact. Consequently it can never recognize more than half-truths and will defend these with the uttermost vigour.

It is essential that in philosophy we should be aware of the method we use, aware of the organ with which we work in the realization of truth, and aware of both its possibilities and limitations.   Intuition and intellect both have their place in the method of philosophy, both have their task and both have their limitations.   The intellect, being the mind functioning in the limitations of the world-image, can and must serve as a *technique* by means of which the artist within, the intuition, can make visible his perception of beauty or of truth.   The intuition, realizing truth in the world of the Real, is the true organ of philosophy, without its creative light the intellect would be but technique without inspiration, lifeless and barren.   On the other hand, the vision of truth which is obtained in the world of the Real, and there alone, needs the technique of the intellect if it is to be conveyed in intelligible language to others or even to ourselves in our everyday consciousness. But we must realize the distinctive duties and functions of intellect and intuition. If we fail to do so we are apt to make of the intellect the discoverer of truth instead of the expositor, and of philosophy an intellectual game, lacking creative life.

The tragedy is that most people are unable to discriminate between the life-giving bread of the intuition and the barren stones of the intellect; in their studies they consume with equal impartiality the one and the other and are as ready to condemn the work of the intuition as ' merely intellectual ' as they are to worship the husks of the intellect as if they were the fruits of the intuition. The intellect is but a skeleton, but to many the rattling of its bones is as sweet a language as the voice of the intuition, they listen with equal reverence to both or else condemn both in the same breath. We shall find many such instances where either the intellect impersonates the intuition or else the voice of the intuition is confused with that of the intellect.

Yet there is far more of intuitive knowledge in the lives of all of us than we realize. How often, when meeting a person or entering a place, do we not have a flash of intuition which, with unerring certainty, leads us to the very heart of things and gives us a far deeper knowledge of the person's character or that of the place than any lengthy process of reasoning or deduction from externals could ever give us. Our first impressions are often of that nature; before a person has even spoken we already know what he will mean to us, whether we like him or not, whether we trust him or would follow him as a leader. All this is intuitive knowledge, and, naturally, in the earlier stages of the development of the intuition apt to be confused with mere prejudice. Yet it plays a far greater role in our lives than we realize. The same holds good for our scientific knowledge, even there it is the flash of intuition which will make the scientist see the truth which then inspires his further experiments. We shall come to realize that philosophy and also science, in so far as they have been truly constructive, have ever used the method of the intuition, though at times unconsciously, and that the intellect is largely but the technique by means of which the realization which the intuition gives is imparted to others or made clear to ourselves.

INTUITIVE KNOWLEDGE AND LOGICAL PROOF

There are two fallacies which at this stage we must face—the fallacy of logical proof leading to truth, and the fallacy that the intuition had no part to play in the truth thus revealed.

The logical method of exposition of any doctrine or theory is one in which each statement follows from the previous one in such a way that what is said in the later statement is contained in principle in the previous ones and nothing new is introduced without being properly linked up. Logic as such, with all its rules and principles, is obedience to a law of mental cause and effect, the entire chain of reasoning being causally connected with certain premises or axiomata, which are thus worked out logically. Logic is the method of the intellect, it is intellectual technique and in itself always unproductive. It is essential, for without it we cannot explain to our ordinary consciousness the truth which the intuition may have seen, but logic never brings forth truth by its own power.

Mathematical reasoning is perhaps the purest example of the logical method; yet in mathematics nothing new is produced as truth and the conclusions to which we come are contained in the principles or axiomata from which we started, even though we may not recognize them there. These axiomata themselves are self-evident to us; we do not feel that they need proving and recognize them intuitively. Thus all mathematical proof is based on principles which cannot be proved and, since, when working out a mathematical problem we never contribute anything new, but rather develop in a process of argumentation certain conclusions from our principles, these conclusions ultimately rest on the intuition which accepted without proof the truth of the axiomata. Hence, if we accept different axiomata as true our mathematics and our conclusions are correspondingly different. Of this the new mathematics presents many examples and its conclusions are necessarily different from those of the Euclidian mathematics and the classical mechanics based on the latter. Hence also the difference between the new physics, based on the new mathematics, and the older physics.

As it is in mathematics so is it also in philosophy—according to the principles from which we start and which we assume as self-evident we reach certain conclusions which appear to be logically true, but which in reality are already conceived in the principles from which we started and which we recognized intuitively. Thus, in philosophy too, logic is the *method of exposition* and as such exceedingly valuable, but it does not lead to truth or produce truth; it is only the intuition which recognizes truth.

We have a craving to see our favourite beliefs logically proved; in fact, most of us are addicted to proof, it is for us the hall-mark of intellectual respectability. A doctrine presented to us without proof is as a stranger without papers or introductions; we look at him askance and can hardly bring ourselves to accept him at his own value as a human being. He too must be ' proved ' for us, he must be linked

up in the chain of known quantities of which our conventional life is composed. A doctrine or truth, presenting
itself without proof on the bare value of its own nobility is
as disturbing a factor to the majority of men as would be the
stranger without name or country. We are afraid of it, it is
to us as an invasion from an unknown world. And such it is,
it *is* an invasion from another world, from the only real world,
the world of Reality ; it is the vision of truth, or intuition,
which, in that world, knows with lightning-like rapidity and
with immediate certainty and which flashes down its message
of truth into the dullness of our illusion-bound intellect.
The intellect stands bewildered at such a visitation from on
high. It is as if a God from high Olympus descended into
a suburban drawing-room ; consternation and a helpless
impotence in the face of the unknown would follow. We
should be afraid of the naked stranger who, from the world of
divinity, descended in our midst and hurriedly clothe him in
the garments of respectability and usher him into the world
of convention as our cousin from abroad. Thus he is linked
up with our conventional world, he is somebody's son, he
has a name and a country.

In the same surreptitious way does our bewildered intellect
clothe the visiting stranger from on high—Intuition. When
the intuition flashes down into our comfortable and well-
ordered world of logic he is hurriedly clothed in the garments
of logic before our neighbours have seen him and he is
introduced to the expectant world as the logical offspring of
premises well known to them. Then, and then alone, do we
feel that we can safely accept him and shall not be compro-
mised by our association with divinity.

There is not a philosophy of importance that has not known
such visitation from on high, that is not rooted in revelation.
When we read the lives or letters of great philosophers we

find how in their youth, perhaps for many years, they thought about the problems of life, they felt the hunger, the yearning to know, they knew the craving for truth, and with every atom of their being strained towards the unknown. For years they read and studied, if not in the books of men then in the Book of Life, they gathered the raw material out of which the creative mind might build its structure. But the moment came for all of them that, for a brief moment, the veil was lifted and they had their revelation, they experienced living truth. Does not Nietzsche tell us how, when he walked in the woods of Sils-Maria, the heavens opened and the world of truth spoke to him with no little voice ? In such moments, often when the intellect is disengaged and dwells but lightly on life, the vision of the intuition breaks like a flash of lightning upon the darkness of our mental life and we know with utter certainty.

Thus, in the domain of science, there was the moment of illumination in Newton's life while he watched the fall of an apple and found what he had been searching for. No doubt his mind was not dwelling on great and weighty problems at the moment, possibly he was but remembering with contentment some small event of daily life and giving himself over to the serenity of the moment. But it is just in these rare silences of our busy lives that the intuition can speak to us ; it is only when the illusion-bound intellect with its noisy self-assertion is quiet for a while that the voice of living truth can be heard. The moment of illumination may well be the outcome of years of mental search, calling forth, as it were, by induction a corresponding activity in the world of the Real, where the untrammeled mind sees the vision and speaks to the mind in prison. But it is always the flash of intuition that shows us the truth and co-ordinates our laboriously gathered intellectual material.

It would show a refreshing sincerity if, some day, we found ourselves able to acknowledge these children of ours, born of the vision of truth, without feeling the urge of respectability to provide them with a legitimate parentage in the world of illusion. We are ashamed of this divine offspring and, if we do bring it forth into the open at all, it is always disguised as the legitimate and inevitable outcome of logical reasoning. Instead of saying at the beginning of our exposition—this have I seen, thus do I know—we put on a false air of innocent ignorance and, after reasoning logically and profoundly through many hundreds of weighty pages, we bring forth as our conclusion the one thing at which we were aiming all the time and with well simulated surprise we stand amazed at the wonderful outcome of our logical reasoning. We have ' proved ' our truth, no trace of the outlaw intuition can be found in our logical exposition ; is it not clear that we started reasoning with an entirely unprejudiced mind and that our doctrine is the logical outcome of our intellectual penetration ? We are like the conjurer who produces the rabbit out of his top hat where he had it concealed all the time, yet it appears as the marvellous result of his magical passes and incantations. Thus our scientists and philosophers often sing their wearisome incantations through many heavy tomes and, like the conjurer, produce their little rabbit at the very end, whereas they had it in their pocket at the beginning of the first chapter.

It is very rare, even in science, that a discovery emerges from experiments which did not tend in that direction. Generally the intuition sees a possible explanation or theory and the experiments which afterwards prove it are but a testing out of the hypothesis or theory already present. Columbus knew that he would reach land sailing West and but proved it by his action.

Yet we must not ever disdain logical exposition and proof. They are valuable, they are essential for a full intellectual appreciation, but they are not productive. It is only when logic and proof claim that they have produced truth and proved that it cannot be otherwise, that we find quarrel with them, that it becomes necessary to put them into the humbler, though equally necessary, position which is theirs by nature. What we need to overcome is our unfounded suspicion of the intuition as the stranger from nowhere ; we must begin to realize, especially in philosophy, that all man has ever thought of any worth in the history of philosophy, he has taught as the result of that inner and direct awareness of truth which we call intuition and not as the prodigious result of wearisome reasoning.

Oriental philosophy has never pretended that it obtained its results by logic and proof, but has ever plainly stated its doctrines, saying—thus I know. In consequence treatises like the *Bhagavad Gita* or the *Tao Teh King* consist of a number of aphorisms or philosophical axiomata which need to be thought and pondered over so that we may understand them fully in their context. A great advantage of this method of philosophizing is the extreme briefness of the books produced ; compared to the ponderous tomes of Western philosophy the brief Eastern treatises are like a refreshing breath from heaven.

I do not know whether we should lose anything of real value by following their methods ; as it is our logical reasoning, our proof and counter proof, never convince any one of a theory which he does not recognize within as true. A conclusive reasoning and apparently irrefutable proof may seem successful for the moment and leave us speechless and acquiescent, but when we come home we are as little convinced as we were before ; all that has been gained was our temporary grudging assent for lack of a suitable counter argument. Hence the futility of debates ; the nimbler wit and readier answer win the day rather than the greater wisdom.

It needs, however, the faculty of discerning and recognizing truth if we are to discriminate between living wisdom, even when coming to us in simple and unassuming garb, and a brilliant but empty intellectual scintillation, even though it appears in all the rich and ornate garments which clever argument and apt reply provide. There are but few in these days of worship of the intellect who are able to recognize the voice of the intuition, and yet, if the intuition is lacking, it cannot be replaced by the crutches of logic and argument.

To many the intuitive recognition of truth as the legitimate way to knowledge is associated with ideas of uncertainty and vagueness. They feel that when a doctrine is presented on the basis of logical argument and conclusive reasoning there is at least something to support it, and, even if the argument or logic may not quite prove the point, yet they provide us with a standard for our approval or condemnation. When, however, all that is presented to us is someone's intuition that this or that is right, how are we to distinguish between a right and a wrong intuition, and how are we to guard ourselves against error ? But, how do we guard ourselves against error at present, while the intuition is but disguised by reasoning and so-called proof ? In philosophy especially we should by now be accustomed to the fact that there is not a doctrine or theory that was not proved at one time as conclusively as it was disproved at another. In reality, when we come to analyze it, we find our judgment at present to be as much an intuitive one as it would be if the doctrine were presented to us on its face value without the pretence of proof. What happens now is that we need not fear to acknowledge our beliefs because they are clad in the respectable garments of logic. It is fear that holds us back, fear to let go the one support which our intellect knows,—argument and logical proof. As the intuition becomes more widely recognized as a legitimate path to knowledge, the uncertainty which at present accompanies its occasional visitations will disappear ; a new organ or function will ever be uncertain in its initial workings. It may reassure us, however, to realize that the greatest teachers of all times have ever presented their conclusions on their inner worth as intuitions ; we do not find a Christ or Buddha proving conclusively that what he says is right, or reasoning out logically his doctrines. They can disdain to use such make-belief of proof and yet they spoke as no man ever spoke, and the hundreds of millions who have followed them have found sufficient conviction in their words through the very spirit of truth that spoke through them. It is only when that spirit is absent that proof and logical reasoning must fill the gap and disguise the emptiness within.

Yet we should ever recognize the value of logical reasoning and intellectual proof as a *technique of communicating* to our fellow-men that which we know within. It enriches the doctrine we bring forward and links it up to all that is familiar and known to us, when it is presented, not as a naked fact, but well reasoned out and supported by evidence. Especially in the domain of science this will ever be the appropriate way of presenting a doctrine or truth, since there the experiment which corroborates the assertions constitutes the proof ; in philosophy such experimental proof is but rarely, if ever, possible.

SCIENCE AND PHILOSOPHY

It is essential that we should understand the respective domains of science and philosophy. Science investigates the world as it appears in our world-image and is not especially concerned with the relation of that world-image to some ultimate reality or the way it is produced in our consciousness. Thus science does not deal with the world of the Real so much as with the appearances or phenomena in our consciousness. It is satisfied to accept this world-image of ours as an independent reality and to forget or even to deny its vital relation to our consciousness. The result is that science to a large extent is still subject to the limitations of our world-image and shares in its illusion. It does not deal with things as they are so much as with things as they appear ; its laws are the shadows of living truth.

We must not make the mistake of confusing the domains of science and philosophy, however much they are mutually illuminating and supply one another's deficiencies. Philosophy deals with the ultimate principles and realities which are the eternal foundation of our world, science deals with the multitude of phenomena in which these principles appear to us ; philosophy deals with the why, science with the how ; philosophy searches for the ultimate nature of being, science is concerned with the functions and workings of this world of forms surrounding us. If science deals with the form-side which our world-image presents, philosophy deals with the life-side to be approached in and through our own consciousness. Introspection is as much the method of the philosopher as observation of outer phenomena is that of the scientist. Thus the two, dealing respectively with phenomena or appearances without and with the realities or final principles within, are supplementary and equally necessary to a full understanding of the world.

It is only a childish intolerance which, on the one hand, would make the scientist disdain philosophy as vain speculation, or on the other hand cause the philosopher to look down upon the work of the scientist as dealing merely with the unreal. For the knowledge of ultimate reality the scientist will ever have to turn to the philosopher as much as the philosopher will have to apply to the scientist for information and knowledge concerning the manifold details of the world of appearances and the way in which things work. Thus we need philosophy for ultimate answers ; science for detailed knowledge and control of natural forces ; and it would be equally wrong to ask of philosophy the exact temperature under which at certain pressure water boils as it would be to ask science the meaning of evil or the relation of this world to its ultimate Cause. Philosophy again is as powerless to produce a motor-car or a telescope as science is when asked the purpose of life, the relation of time and the eternal, or the measure of freedom of the human will. Mutual contempt of philosophy and science is as harmful as it is unfounded, but we must ever be on our guard against asking of one a question belonging to the domain of the other. A scientific answer to a philosophical question will necessarily be unsatisfactory and beside the point, just as a philosophical solution to a scientific question would be empty of meaning and scientifically valueless. We honour both best by understanding their respective spheres of knowledge and by co-ordinating them to their greatest benefit, never by confusing their respective tasks.

In mediaeval times science and philosophy were one in a confusion detrimental to the development of both ; since the time of Bacon science and philosophy diverged more and more until in the nineteenth century they seemed mutually exclusive ; now, in the twentieth century they are to be co-ordinated, no longer confused as in the Middle Ages, but seen in a unity in which each has its own task and function, well defined and distinguished from that of the other.

OCCULTISM AND MYSTICISM

It is interesting to see how the essential difference and mutually supplementary character of philosophy and science are evident also in their respective extensions into mysticism and occultism. It is in modern Theosophy that we find the clearest presentation of these two, especially of the latter—occultism.

The claim of occultism is that this physical world is not the only world which can be investigated scientifically ; it teaches that there are worlds of subtler matter which can be explored scientifically by those who have developed the faculties of perception in those worlds, what we might call the occult senses, such as clairvoyance at different levels, clairaudience and other similar faculties.

There is nothing improbable or impossible in an extension of sense-perception beyond the limits of our normal five senses. It is common knowledge that even within the range of the usual senses there are appreciable differences with regard to the limits of perception ; some will hear a more rapid vibration of the air as sound, or see a more rapid vibration of the ether as light than others. And apart from the greater sensitiveness in ordinary perception there is the evidence of so-called transposition of the ordinary sense-functions to almost any part of the body. Thus Richet tells in his work *Thirty Years of Psychical Research* (p. 186 ff.) of the case of a person who, in a state of hypnosis, had the faculty of sight temporarily localized in the finger-tips, so that she could read a page of print with the hands instead of with the eyes. This and similar experiments point to the possibility of sense-perception without the use of the ordinary five senses, and to the existence of a sixth sense not dependent upon the physical sense-organs.

We ourselves, in ordinary life cannot fail to come across instances, where a knowledge of events is obtained when there is no sense-evidence whatsoever to provide it. The knowledge of the illness or death of a friend far away, of an accident or catastrophe taking place at a distance, or even of an event to take place in the future, is thus obtained by means of an inner sense which transcends the five physical senses. Finally there is the evidence of those who claim to have developed consciously senses not normally developed in man, but presumably capable of development by those who follow the necessary training.

Only with a more widespread development of occult faculties can occultism become science, the science of worlds of matter subtler than the physical. Meanwhile we must classify whatever is produced along lines of occult investigation as belonging to the domain of science rather than to that of philosophy. Like science occultism is the investigation of an outside world or of outside worlds in their multiplicity of forms and colours, presented in dimensions of time and space. As such it is the observation and investigation of a world-image ; as ordinary science explores the physical world-image so does occultism attempt to explore an etheric, astral or mental world-image. It, therefore, has the same possibilities and limitations which science has, it leads to a knowledge of the *how* not of the *why* of things, it leads to knowledge and control of the outer worlds, not to knowledge of ultimate principles.

Occultism, as little as science, has an answer to give to ultimate questions ; it may show us the working and functioning of things—the how—somewhat further than ordinary science can, it may show the way things appear in a world-image beyond the merely physical world-image, but essentially it is not the task of either science or occultism to answer

final questions. To expect such things of them is to misunderstand their mission and their possibility ; we do not
expect an electric lamp to produce music or a piano to give
light. Each has its own power and value and it would be
ignorance on our part and not unsufficiency on theirs if we
expect the wrong thing from them and they fail to supply it.

It is important to understand this, especially where in
modern theosophy the claim is so often made for occultism
that it offers a philosophy and answers the problems of life.
It does not offer a philosophy of life any more than science
does, and if we expect occultism to answer fundamental
problems we misunderstand its function. Occultism offers
an extension of science into subtler worlds, mainly the world
of emotions and the world of thought, but its investigations
are investigations of a world-image, not experience of reality.

This does not in any way belittle the scope of occultism, it
merely corrects a misunderstanding which leads to absurdity.
We shall, in later chapters, have occasion to point out various
instances where the interesting and valuable products of
occult investigation are mistaken for philosophical truths and
presented as answering ultimate questions. This confusion
is detrimental to the development of occultism since, thus,
claims are made on its behalf which it can never fulfil.
Occultism has no more an answer for such problems as the
nature of evil, the freedom of the will, the justice of life or the
relation of consciousness to matter, than science. If we
would pursue these metaphysical questions we must follow
a different line.

Just as in modern theosophy we find occultism or psychism
presented as an extension of science so do we find a philosophical mysticism presented as an extension of philosophy.
The fundamental doctrine of theosophy, that of the unity of
all life, belongs to this domain of philosophical mysticism ;

no clairvoyant investigation at whatsoever level can ever *observe* the unity of life.

In its philosophical mysticism theosophy transcends intellectual speculation and leads to the experience of reality. In this it shows its kinship with Neo-Platonic mysticism ; Plotinus too proclaimed that it is possible for philosophy to be more than an intellectual structure, that it is possible to *experience* as inner realities those things which ordinary philosophy would present as intellectual beliefs. Thus he says, (*Ennead* VI., 9, 4.).

> Plato says of Unity that it is unspeakable and indescribable. Nevertheless we speak of it, we write about it, but only to excite our souls by our discussions, and to direct them towards this divine spectacle, just as one might point out the road to somebody who desired to see some object. Instruction, indeed, goes as far as showing the road, and guiding us in the way ; but to obtain the vision of the Divinity is the work suitable to him who desires to obtain it.

Intellectual philosophy may come to the conclusion that there is a world of reality of which our everyday world is but the image produced in our consciousness ; philosophical mysticism goes one step further and claims that it is possible for man to enter that world of reality and *experience* living truth. Again, not content with recognizing, as some philosophies do, that in our normal consciousness we are subject to illusion, philosophical mysticism claims the power for man *to conquer this illusion and establish himself in Reality*. Thus, where philosophy believes, philosophical mysticism experiences, it transcends belief in being.

In this way philosophical mysticism is as legitimate an extension of ordinary philosophy as occultism or psychism is of ordinary science. It is interesting to see how the evolutionary tendencies of modern philosophy are towards this philosophical mysticism, even though it may not be mentioned by that name. The recognition of the intuition in Bergson's philosophy as a method of knowledge beyond the intellect ; the impatience with intellectual systems of philosophy into which life is expected to fit and the attempt at a philosophy which is creative, vital and based on experience, such as we find in the work of Count Keyserling ; the interest of many philosophers in the new mathematics, so evident in Bertrand Russell's work ; and finally, a definitely mystical philosophy like that of Ouspensky in his *Tertium Organum*, all these are signs of the gradual evolution from a merely intellectual philosophy into a philosophy of intuition and experience.

In modern theosophy it is through its aspect as philosophical mysticism that we must approach ultimate questions. The doctrine of theosophy with regard to the illusion or *maya* of the phenomenal worlds, its teaching that the goal of life is the attaining of ultimate reality which can be reached by a process of inner realization, above all its doctrine of the unity of life and of universal brotherhood, all these belong to theosophy as philosophical mysticism. As such it truly offers a philosophy of life ; as such it leads to the experience of the mystery of life, as such it may help us with regard to problems such as that of the ultimate justice of life, the origin of evil and suffering, or the relation of life to form or of soul to body. But as such it does not and cannot ever answer questions with regard to the detailed forms of our world-image, whether physical, emotional or mental ; this detailed knowledge, as well as the knowledge of the way in which things work, belongs to science and its extension—occultism.

In theosophical literature there is as yet no clear understanding of and discrimination between these two aspects of its teaching—the occult-scientific and the mystic-philosophical, and consequently we often meet with philosophical heresies on the one hand, where the results of occult investigation are produced as the answers to philosophical questions, and scientific heresies on the other hand, where questions which can only be answered by a precise and scientific occultism are answered by philosophical or mystical statements. The result is that the true values of theosophy are obscured both in the eyes of the scientist and of the philosopher, and that the progress of theosophical investigation is impeded.

It is curious to see how through history the scientific and the philosophical type and also the mystic and the occultist have misunderstood and even opposed one another. The age-long struggle between religion and science is rooted in that misunderstanding, a misunderstanding accentuated when religion becomes a dogmatic orthodoxy and science an equally dogmatic materialism, such as they were a century ago. In principle we find the antithesis of the two types already in the disapproval on the part of Plotinus, the philosophical mystic, of the writings of the Gnostics, whose tendencies were definitely in the direction of occultism. In more recent times we find a similar, though more open, warfare between the philosophical mysticism of the Cambridge Platonists of the seventeenth century and the occultism of the Rosicrucians and Alchemists of that period. When we study the series of polemical pamphlets interchanged between Henry More, the Platonist, and Thomas Vaughan, known as Eugenius Philalethes, the famous Rosicrucian, we are struck not only by the misunderstanding of each other's methods and contributions to knowledge, but by the ill concealed bitterness and the mutual contempt which even the titles of their pamphlets manifest. Yet both were men of outstanding nobility of character and erudition and, seeing the extent of their antagonism, we can well imagine what would happen in the case of lesser representatives on both sides.

We must learn to see the two—philosophy and science—as well as their extensions, mysticism and occultism, co-ordinated in a higher unity without confusing their characteristic methods and aims. The methods of science and occultism will ever be accurate observation by means of our senses and the intellectual elaboration of these sense-data; the method of philosophy and of philosophical mysticism will ever be that of the intuition or realization in consciousness. And it is that method of realization which we shall have to use in our exploration of the world of the Real.

CHAPTER FOUR

THE ABSOLUTE AND THE RELATIVE

There is an endless world, O my Brother ! and there is the
Nameless Being, of whom nought can be said.
Only he knows it who has reached that region : it is other than
all that is heard and said.
No form, no body, no length, no breadth is seen there : how can
I tell you that which it is ?

—KABIR, *Tagore*, 76.

THE REALIZATION OF THE ABSOLUTE

THE world of the Real, which we enter when we pass through
our centre of consciousness, is the Absolute, it is That
beyond and beside which nothing exists. In a way it is not
even right to speak of a world which we enter. First of all
it is not a world, secondly we do not really enter it and finally
it is not really we who enter that world. No phraseology
derived from the experience of our world-image can fit the
Absolute, ultimate Reality. Down here we speak of a
' world ' and the word immediately conveys a conception of
a universe arranged around us, outside us, with spatial
separation between its creatures and objects, changing,
growing and evolving in time. In that sense the Absolute
is not a world ; if, however, we call it ' world ' it is the one
and only World that exists, which ever did exist or ever can
exist. Let us then for a moment call it neither world nor
state of consciousness or being, nor by any name derived
from experience in our world-image consciousness. It is
That, the Absolute, and if in speaking about It we must of
necessity use words derived from our common experience,

let it always be understood that the insufficiency of such words is recognized and felt, but that the impossibility of an adequate language makes it necessary to take our refuge in the insufficient.

When we say that it is not really *we* who enter that world something is indicated which must be experienced in order to be known. When we emerge through our centre of consciousness, the Void in which there is no content of consciousness, and when we ' emerge on the other side,' we do not enter something which we are not, but we are That which we realize on the other side of this centre of consciousness. We are It in its entirety, we are It fully and wholly, we are It in all its possible manifestations, in all that It is, has been or can be, for in It time is eternity. Thus it is not really correct to speak any longer of ' I ' or ' we ' ; we truly are That and lose for the time being all consciousness of being a separate creature, of being someone. That is why *even the term ' consciousness ' is no longer valid* for the realization of the Absolute, the nearest expression we can use for it is ' being.' Consciousness always implies someone who is conscious of something ; in the word ' consciousness ' there is implied a consciousness and a content of the consciousness, something of which we are aware. Therefore the word consciousness seems futile when used for that ultimate Reality, we there gain a realization in which we are all that is and our knowing is being.

HOW IS THE ABSOLUTE KNOWN ?

What right have we to give the name ' Absolute ' to that which we realize when emerging through our centre of consciousness, how do we know that it is not a world only relatively more real than our world-image, how can we term it absolute Reality ?

Let us first realize that what we experience is not something which differs in quantity or greatness or measure from the world-image we know in our daily consciousness ; it is not something greater, more glorious, more beautiful or more comprehensive, it is utterly and entirely different. Where our world image presents itself to us decked in all the rich variety of sense-qualities, with colour and sound, taste, smell and touch, with form and shape, with measures of space and time, with a multiplicity of separate creatures and objects, all distinct one from the other and dependent on one another, interrelated, this Reality which we experience shows nothing of all that. If we experienced a world only relatively more real than our world-image there would be still some characteristics corresponding at a higher level to our world-image ; we might see more beautiful, more ethereal colours, hear more wonderful sounds, find ourselves in the midst of greater beauty and fulness of life. But here in the world of the Real there is no longer a universe surrounding us, there is no longer separateness, there are no longer the qualities which form the garment of our world-image ; we have become That which is pure Unity, containing all multiplicity, though not showing any separateness.

Here the intellect, bound as it is to the illusions of the world-image, fails us ; to the intellect the world may seem one *or* many, but cannot be both at the same time. The realities of the Absolute must always be paradoxes to the intellect and whatever is explained about them intellectually will always lead to misunderstanding. Perhaps an image may help us to understand, though, like all images and comparisons, it must necessarily be insufficient and even somewhat misleading.

When we consider the number one in arithmetic that number is a unity, it is entirely and homogeneously one. Yet we can also think of that number one as being composed of a vast number of fractions ; we can divide it again and again into millions of fractions of different values until we are bewildered by the seemingly endless multitude of the parts. Yet, at the same time, the number one has not been touched at all in its serene unity ; it is ever one, and yet at the same time it is ever these countless fractions ; they are contained in it, hidden in it, present in it and one with it. We cannot say that there are two different things, a unity on the one side and a multiplicity of fractions on the other, no, the two are one and it depends on the way in which we consider the number one whether we shall see it as unity or multiplicity. When we see it as unity, there is no interaction, there is no relation of part to part, there is no relativity. In this sense the number one may be compared to the Absolute, that which is determined in, by and through itself and is not related to anything else. Yet, the Absolute is all the time the multiplicity of all things ; unchanged and eternally serene in Itself, It yet contains within Itself all that ever has been or can be ; It is all that eternally. When we thus experience reality as multiplicity, as the manifoldness of different things, we can speak of relation between one thing and another, then we are in the realm of relativity.

In this world of relativity each relative thing is related to all else ; there is not an atom in this universe of mine to which I am not related, even though I may not be conscious of the relation. I have no existence at all as a separate creature, though I may at times imagine myself as such ; rather am I part of an intricate web of relativity in which all things mutually determine one another. The standpoint of each relative thing in this world of relativity must necessarily always be relative ; whatever it sees is seen from that standpoint which necessarily has a certain relation to all other things. No two standpoints can ever be the same, all standpoints are different and therefore the outlook from each standpoint is different from all others—all truth is relative in the world of relativity. Only then can we speak of absolute truth in the world of relativity when we can discount the element of relativity in each relative outlook, that is to say, when, instead of fondly imagining our relative viewpoint to show absolute truth we can take into account the relativity of our standpoint and deduct that, as it were, from our outlook, leaving a truth which is no longer relative. Thus we come to this apparently paradoxical conclusion, that we are only able to approach absolute truth when we can realize our truth as relative truth ; only the theory of relativity makes it possible to formulate scientific law in an absolute and no longer in a relative way.

There can never be freedom for the relative, since every relative thing is at least partially determined by all else that is relative. Only the Absolute is free since there is naught beside It. There is no interaction between the Absolute and the relative ; the relative thing can only be related to other relative things. Relation denotes relativity, and the Absolute has no relation to anything because It is all things. Its only relation to the relative is that the relative as a whole is the Absolute, but there is never the possibility of a relation between *a* relative thing or being and the Absolute.

Since there is no relation between the relative and the Absolute, except in so far as the Absolute is the relative in its entirety, we are no longer the relative when we realize the Absolute, that is to say we are no longer ' we ' or 'I ' when we are That. That is why in Buddhism the realization of the Absolute is called *Nirvana*, literally the ' going out ' or ' becoming extinct,' since from the standpoint of the separate self it means the end of all things, though from the standpoint of reality it means the beginning of all things. Nirvana is the extinction of the craving to be the relative thing and thereby the extinction of the relative as such in the realization of the Absolute. We are as justified to say that *we become the Absolute*, that the dewdrop becomes the shining sea, as we are in saying that the dewdrop is lost when slipping into the sea, that *we are annihilated when realizing the Absolute*. It will ever be impossible to express reality in the language of our world-image.

Since there is no relation possible between a relative thing and the Absolute there is no such thing as a worship of the Absolute, devotion to the Absolute, or response from the Absolute to a worshipping being ; all this is a philosophical impossibility and the very suggestion implies a lack of understanding. If we desire to give the name ' God ' to the Absolute—and it does not really matter what name we give to That—let it be well understood that it can never be the God to whom we pray, whom we invoke, whom we worship, whom we speak of as loving or kind, whom we look upon as Creator of the universe. Magnificent as the conception of such a Deity may be, infinitely fertile as it has been and must ever be in calling forth the noblest emotions and the highest endeavour, we must never for a moment confuse it with That, compared to which even this Deity is relative.

Our universe as such is relative, limited and finite and so is the ensouling Life or the Deity whose creation we suppose this universe to be. The God of Christianity, the Trinity of Father, Son and Holy Ghost, is the Deity of our universe, the Deity to whom we can pray and who is Love. Even so is the *Logos* of theosophical doctrine ; the three Logoi of whom modern theosophy speaks are identical with the Christian Trinity, but they are not That, not the Absolute ; the Logos too, though beyond our human understanding, is

yet *a* Being, not Being. The great difference between
Buddhism and Christianity is that where Buddhism is
concerned with That, with the Absolute, Christianity speaks
of the Deity of our universe. Hence in Buddhism no mention
of God, no worship of God and in Christianity a wonderful
system of ceremonial worship and devotion to the God of our
universe.

We must not make the mistake of looking upon the Absolute as one step higher than the Deity of a universe ; it is
not as if there were first humanity, then superhuman beings
and those who govern our human evolution, then the Deity of
our universe and then—if we ascend still very much higher—
the Absolute. When the Hindu speaks of the God of this
universe as *Brahma* and of the Absolute as *Parabrahman* we
should misunderstand his meaning if we thought of Parabrahman as a magnification and glorification of Brahma. In
some ways the Absolute is infinitely nearer to us than the
Deity of a universe, in another way It is infinitely greater.
Yet to say that It is greater would denote a greater measure
of the same Being or reality and It is not such. It is of such
a nature that It cannot even be compared to the greatest
Being in the world of the relative, there is nothing to which
It can ever be compared.

Sometimes we hear people say, ' I do not attempt to understand the Absolute ; even the Deity of a universe is far
beyond my understanding, and how can I hope to know
anything of the Absolute which is still greater.' Such an
attitude, in a seeming humility, yet shows misunderstanding
and misconception. If the Deity of our universe is seen
along an ever ascending line of ever increasing greatness and
perfection, the attitude spoken of implies that, if we ascend
that line still further and mount still higher, we may some
day reach the Absolute, which is absurd. In the world of

the relative truly there is always greatness beyond greatness, and when we have reached the greatest, noblest we know or dimly apprehend, yet wider vistas open up before us and we see a greatness undreamt of at our previous level of understanding. But not of such is the Absolute. It is not great; to call It great would be misunderstanding the reality of the Absolute. How can we call anything great when there is nothing else to compare to it in size or in fullness of manifestation; there is no comparison where there is only the One; there is no greatness and there is no smallness. We do not reach the Absolute by ascending or hoping to ascend some day beyond even the greatest Being whom we can now dimly see on our spiritual horizon; the way to the Absolute is not along that ever ascending line of greater and greater, of more and more, of nobler and nobler; we can reach the Absolute at the very point where we are now, just as much or just as little as we can reach It when we are the greatest Being in the world of relativity. It is rather as if, instead of continuing the endless process of ever ascending greatness, of ever increasing perfection we went by a different dimension altogether and disappeared out of the realm of change and growth and evolution into that of changeless and ever abiding Being, Nirvana. It is as if, instead of moving along a certain path, ascending in a certain direction, we were to move *within*, into the very point where we find ourselves and, through that, reached the Absolute. That is what does happen to us when we reach It through the centre of our consciousness. We do not aspire, ascend, or strain towards something greater than we are, we disappear into ourselves and, through ourselves as the relative, reach the Absolute which is at every point of the relative. Magnificent though the conception of spiritual evolution is, utterly true though it is for our world-image consciousness, yet to one who has seen the Vision of That which is eternal and which neither changes nor evolves, containing as it does all change and all evolution, the highest dreams of evolutionary progress become but—dreams.

Returning then to our question, how we know that this world of the Real is the Absolute, we can answer—it is by experiencing just that which is characteristic of the Absolute. We have seen that it is only in the relative consciousness that the interpretation of absolute Reality into sense-qualities, time and space measures is affected. Reality itself is devoid of all that, yet contains the fulness of it. That which we become in reaching reality is of this nature; it has no qualities, yet is that which produces qualities in the relative consciousness. It is not time, yet it is that which, when realized by the relative consciousness, is experienced as time with its illusory past and future; it is not space nor distance, yet contains within itself that which, when appreciated and interpreted by the relative consciousness, becomes space in our world-image. Again, That which we become is not related to anything else; It is everything and everything is within It. When we are That we do not feel greater than we are in our ordinary consciousness, not increased, not more real when compared to that reality of every day; we have entirely left the world of the relative and are That which knows *no relativity and no comparison*. In That we are not in relation to anything else, since we are all things; hence here alone is freedom, since there is nothing outside to cause limitation.

That which we experience is changeless, though containing all change, and as such neither increases nor decreases. Being unchanging it is all that we call past and all that we call future, these are present in it as an eternal Reality. There alone is peace, there alone there can never be the desire for more or greater or nobler; It is All. The absence of all relativity, of all relationships denotes that which we call the Absolute; it is not dependent upon anything else because it is the Alone. It is the ' one dark Truth ' of which the Mystic speaks, the final Mystery for which there is no explanation, since there is naught to explain it with. If the unphilosophical mind were to ask: Why the Absolute? and Whence the Absolute? the unchanging Voice of that which is eternal and unchanging would give him the answer, could he but realize it. The Absolute is its own explanation, its own cause, its own fulfilment and its own realization. It is That.

ABSOLUTE AND RELATIVE IN RELIGION

In the light of the foregoing the difference between science and philosophy, or between occultism and mysticism stands out clearly; the aims of science and occultism lie in the world of the relative, those of philosophy and mysticism in the Absolute; science and occultism are content to investigate the ways in which the relative appears to the relative and to gain power and control in the world of relativity; philosophy and mysticism know no peace until they reach that ultimate Reality which has no beyond; to them reality means either the Absolute or nothing at all. Once again we can see how foolish it is to extol one above the other; a complete knowledge implies knowledge of the relative as well as realization of the Absolute.

In matters of religion the relative outlook shows man as a growing, evolving being with those greater than himself ahead, those less than himself behind. It shows a world, beginning and ending, created, thought or imagined by a Deity who is the informing life of this universe. Thus, in religious matters, occultism speaks to us of a hierarchy of ever evolving beings, a seemingly endless ladder of perfection of which none has ever beheld the topmost rung. The Deity of occultism is the great Being upon whom we look as Creator of this universe; Him we can worship and adore, to Him devotion can rise up and from Him benediction can descend. Thus the occultist will stress the scientific value of ceremonial magic which in this world of the relative unites man closer to the God of His universe and provides a method of pouring out divine creative Energy.

How different is the religious aspect of philosophical mysticism; equally valuable and equally justified, but different in aims and methods. The philosophical mystic does not speak much of a hierarchy of ever greater and greater beings, for him there is but one goal, one achievement—the Absolute. That is the God of the philosophical mystic, a God who is not Creator of the universe but who is eternally all universes, a God to whom no man can pray, but whom we *are* when we reach Reality. To Him no adoration can ascend, from Him no benediction descends to man. He is unchanging eternal Peace, the Alone beyond which naught is. This eternal Peace of the Absolute is the Buddhist Nirvana; Nirvana, as taught by the Buddha, is not the evolution into greater power and knowledge, but the passing out of evolution into an Eternal in which is no suffering, no unsatisfied craving because there is no separateness, no ' I,' no possibility of incompleteness. Nirvana thus is not a crowning glory in an ascending scale of ever increasing divine experiences, it is the radical and fundamental departure from all that is relative into the Absolute.

If we compare Christianity and Buddhism we cannot help but feel that Buddhism is more the religion of the Absolute, Christianity that of the Relative. The God of Christianity is the Triune Deity of this universe rather than the Absolute, even though, in the experiences of Christian mystics we, at times, find God as the ultimate Reality. Hence also the difference in ideals between the Buddhist Nirvana and the Christian Kingdom of God ; in the attaining of Nirvana the realm of relativity is left for the eternal peace of the Absolute, in the Kingdom of God we see a religious ideal which is rather a deification of the world of relativity in a life of perfect love. In the love of the Christian we see the endeavour to realize the unity of divine life *in* the world of relativity, in the Nirvana of the Buddhist the departure from relativity for the peace of the Absolute. We should not make the mistake of trying to judge which ideal is better or nobler, rather should we rejoice that there is a religion which shows the divine in the relative, like Christianity, and also a religion like Buddhism which shows the divine as the Absolute.

Christianity is a ritualistic religion, there is no ceremonial so complete and deeply valuable as the Christian ; in Buddhism we in vain look for ceremonial. In a Buddhist temple we may lay a few flowers in front of the image of the Buddha, we may place a candle or burning light in front of the shrine in token of reverence, but beyond that there is no ritual. Neither do we find in Buddhism a conception of God as we do in Christianity, hence Buddhism has often been termed atheistic. Yet we can understand why there is no place in Buddhism for a Deity as in Christianity, when we realize that for Buddhism, as the religion of the philosophical mystic, there is no reality short of the Absolute and no peace short of Nirvana. We should not fear such differences in religion, true tolerance tries to recognize the value of each religion as a characteristic manifestation of living truth which necessarily implies essential differences between the different religions ; to smooth out these differences until they all appear to be the same would mean a levelling down of a rich variety to the dead monotony of similarity. True tolerance does not lie in blindness to characteristic differences, but rather in understanding why these differences exist and why they are valuable in the unity of universal religion.

Naturally we find different types of men in each of the great religions; thus there are Christians to whom ceremonial is the breath of life and whose worship centres round the invocation and descent of divine grace and power in the Eucharist, and, on the other hand, there are those in the Christian religion to whom ceremonial seems but an obstacle and for whom the path to reality is one of renunciation of externals rather than one of the emphasis of external means in ceremonial worship. We must not confuse this with the contempt of ceremonial worship which we find sometimes in Protestant Christianity and which often is based not so much on intensity of mystical endeavour as on the inability to appreciate aught but an intellectual dogmatism. On the other hand, in Roman Catholicism, we at times meet with a ceremonialism which is merely traditional and claims to be essential to man's salvation and to his life in the world of relativity. Yet, even at these levels the difference between mystical endeavour and occult methods appears and often leads to misunderstanding and antagonism.

To the occultist the philosophical mystic's realization of the Absolute will seem to be a baseless presumption; to him, working as he is in the world of relativity the Absolute means but a Being still greater than the Deity of his universe, a yet higher level, of still greater power and glory. He would fail to understand that the mystic's achievement does not lie in the attaining of ever greater glory, but in leaving the world of the relative altogether and in entering That, with regard to which words like power and glory, greatness and wisdom have no meaning. The occultist would see the Absolute as part of his world of relativity, the very highest and noblest part it is true, but yet part of it. But the Absolute cannot be expressed in terms of relativity, the quadrature of the circle is impossible. On the other hand the philosophical mystic at times fails to recognize the value of that worship which sees God in the world of the relative and adores him as a Being, great and loving, tender and wise.

Absolute and relative both have their place in religion ; for our world of relativity a religion of relativity is of daily value, yet if we would attain to ultimate Reality we must seek the Absolute and its realization.

THE ABSOLUTE AND THE RELATIVE IN MAN

Relativity is but another way of considering the Absolute ; the Absolute is one and many simultaneously, it is the infinitude of fractions as well as the unity of which all fractions are part. Yet there are not two worlds, one of relativity and one of the Absolute ; there is but one world of ultimate Reality, the Absolute, which, when approached in its multiplicity is the relative. This multiplicity of all that ever was or can be is the Absolute and therefore the infinitely small is as essential to the unity of all things as the infinitely great ; not a grain of dust could ever be taken away from that totality of things, since it is not a detached object, but an inseparable part of a living Unity.

Plotinus illustrates the unity of Absolute and Relative in the following passage from *Ennead* iv. 2, where he says :

On the other hand, there exists another kind of essence (' being '), whose nature differs from the preceding (entirely divisible things), which admits of no division, and is neither divided nor divisible. This has no extension, not even in thought. It does not need to be in any place, and is not either partially or wholly contained in any other being. If we dare say so, it hovers simultaneously over all beings, not that it needs to be built up on them, but because it is indispensable to the existence of all. It is ever identical with itself, and is the common support of all that is below it. It is as in the circle, where the centre, remaining immovable in itself, nevertheless is the origin of all the radii originating there, and drawing their existence thence.

The Absolute, indeed, contains within itself all relativity as the circle contains within itself the infinitude of rays from centre to circumference. Each ray is connected with the centre, proceeds from the centre and in the centre all rays are one. On the circumference, however, they are many ; while there is unity in the centre of the circle there is multiplicity and separateness on the circumference. Thus in the circle, too, unity and multiplicity are contained ; in the realization of the Absolute we have all multiplicity within us as a unity, just as, from the centre of the circle we see all rays, see the whole circle and its multiplicity in unity. On the circumference, however, where we do not realize the centre which binds all, we may have the illusion that all rays, which we only know at their furthest extension, are separate ; the circumference is the realm of relativity. The philosophical mystic travels along his ray to the centre and from there understands the circle as a whole in one comprehensive realization ; the occultist and scientist explore along the circumference and there gain a detailed knowledge of the world of multiplicity.

Every human being, every created thing is as a ray going forth from the centre of the eternal Circle to its circumference. In the centre, whence it issues forth, it is one with all other rays and realizes itself to be the whole ; it is all things, it is the Absolute. Where it touches the circumference it is but one of many and instead of realizing itself as the Absolute it gazes upon the world of multiplicity, the world of relativity, where problems arise since the unity of life is

lost. Thus in ourselves we are the great mystery, absolute
and relative simultaneously ; when we look within, piercing
through our own consciousness, we can realize ultimate
Reality and cease to be ourselves by being That which is all
things ; on the other hand, when we feel ourselves only as
the separate ray, we are surrounded by the multitude of other
created things and subject to the illusion of separateness,
bringing with it the externalizing of our world-image and its
objectivation as an independent reality. Our consciousness
has as it were two windows, one through which we gaze on
our own world-image and behold multiplicity in the world
of the relative and another through which we emerge into
the world of the Real, where we cease to be the relative and
are the Absolute. These two apparently contradictory facts
form the paradox in the unity of our human nature ; in
ourselves takes place that mystery which cannot be accomplished by any other means—the quadrature of the
circle ; in us the Eternal becomes time, the Absolute the
relative.

We must guard against the illusion of duality, as if there
were on the one hand the Absolute and on the other the
relative, which then are synthesized in a higher unity. This
idea is but an example of intellectual fallacy and, like most
fallacies, is glibly accepted by many, especially when demonstrated by a symbol like that which we have just used, the
circle. How easy it is to say that the centre of the circle
symbolizes the Absolute, the circumference the relative and
the two are aspects of the supreme Reality. Yet this would
be entirely wrong, a mere intellectual superficiality. There
is but one Reality, the Absolute, which we may, if we wish
to do so, symbolize by the circle containing within itself the
multitude of rays. A circle, however, is not a combination
of centre and circumference, but is essentially radiation from

a point. That is the reality of the circle, to be seen only from the centre ; thus also the Absolute can be realized only from the Centre where the entire Circle is seen in its multiplicity of rays. The world-view of the separate ray which has travelled away from the common Centre is the relative view ; surrounded by the many other rays the individual ray feels itself as separate amongst other creatures and is conscious of a world of relativity. But the Absolute is ever That beyond and beside which naught is and not in any way the opposite of the relative. *The relative is eternally contained within the Absolute.*

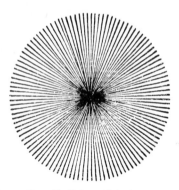

DIAGRAM TWO.—The Circle as radiation from a point.

In the world of relativity we can never come to the realization of truth, since there we are always subject to the illusions due to the objectivation of our world-image. The relative cannot express the Absolute, and ultimate reality or living truth must ever remain a paradox to the intellect which is subject to the world-image. It is only in the world of the Absolute that we can come to a realization of truth and can know Reality by becoming it.

WRONG PROBLEMS IN PHILOSOPHY

When we analyze some of the illusory features of our world-image consciousness we can see why a realization of living truth is impossible in that consciousness and why every question asked from that state of consciousness must be permeated by the illusion to which it is subject. The multiplicity which in the Absolute is seen as a unity appears as separateness in my externalized world-image ; I am conscious of myself as centre of a surrounding world and feel myself as ' I ' with regard to that world as ' not I.' Such is the predominant characteristic of my world-image consciousness—the I not-I illusion. Everything in my daily experience is coloured by that and subject to that, whatever I think or feel, whatever I do or experience, whatever I ask or answer is part of that dual structure : my consciousness of being I, surrounded by a world which is not I. The most dangerous part of this illusion is that I am not aware of it and am accustomed to ask questions of a philosophical nature without realizing for a moment that they are coloured and vitiated by the illusion which accompanies my consciousness in the world of the relative.

In addition to this dualistic illusion which colours all my questioning and thinking in the world of the relative there are my space and time illusions ; that which is an abiding and ever-present reality in the Absolute becomes a past-present-future development in my world-image. I objectivate this way of experiencing the eternal as a succession of events and call this objectivation ' time,' considering it as a scroll on which events are written. Then, forgetting that this particular time-structure of my world-image is but *my* way of interpreting ever-present reality, I unconsciously weave it into the texture of all my thoughts and questions, and all the problems which my imprisoned intellect can ask are impregnated by that illusion. Thus all questions in which the problem of the beginning or the end of time or of the relation of past and future to the present enters, are incapable of being answered since they have an element of illusion in themselves.

In a similar way distance in space and the three dimensions of my space world are *my* interpretation, in my world-image, of that which, in the Absolute, may be thought of as a mathematical point. There is no space in the world of the Real, though there is that which I interpret in dimensions of space and time. The space illusion of my world-image also colours my thinking and feeling without my realizing that it does so ; I never doubt that I am ' here ' and that someone else is ' there,' at a distance of ten yards from me. Yet this is only the appearance in my world-image of that which in the Absolute is not spatially distant, and consequently, when I ask a philosophical question in which the illusion of an objective space is implied, I shall naturally find these questions impossible to answer since they are wrong in themselves.

As long as we, in philosophy, ask questions concerning reality, while we are bound in the illusion of our relative standpoint, and then try to deal with these faulty questions by means of the intellect, which is the mind functioning in the realm of relativity, it is quite impossible to come to a realization of living truth. At the very best we can hope to get an answer to our wrong question, which answer, since the question was wrong must necessarily be wrong also and therefore without value. The agnostic is at least safer in declaring that these questions cannot be answered, that man cannot know ultimate things. This may not be true, but at least it safeguards us from these pseudo-answers which do but act as mental soporifics. When the agnostic says, ' we cannot know,' he is right if he adds the words ' by the aid of our intellect,' since the intellect is the instrument for observation in the world of relativity, and fails us when we desire to attain reality. Then the intuition alone can serve as a way to knowledge, the intuition being the experience of reality in our being; but both intellect and intuition are necessarily incapable of answering questions which are wrong in themselves. To answer such is but to prove our ignorance.

We can escape from the *circulus vitiosus* of wrong question and wrong answer only by recognizing that the questions are asked from the standpoint of illusion and that the intellect is bound to this same illusion. It is only when we surrender both and leave all trappings of the world of relativity behind that we can enter the world of the Real and there experience Reality, which does not answer the wrong questions, but rather sweeps them aside and gives us a realization of living truth instead, in the light of which the very questions become absurd. ' The soul answers never by words, but by the thing itself that is inquired after,' says Emerson. We do not gain an answer in so many words, but experience a living reality which shows the absurdity of the wrong question and makes a further answer superfluous.

ESOTERIC AND EXOTERIC

The realization of the Absolute, of living truth, is a supreme reality, which can never be voiced in the language of the intellect. In that sense it is *esoteric* as compared to teaching which can be intellectually explained and which consequently is *exoteric*. The term esoteric knowledge or esoteric teaching is often used for a body of information in the hands of some select group of students who know this teaching and for some reason or other do not consider it right to make it public. Such teaching is secret, since it is kept only for the few, but it is not esoteric in the true sense of the word. True esoteric knowledge is not knowledge which we for some good reason *refuse* to make public, but rather knowledge which no one *can* make public, since it cannot be expressed, since there is no language to explain it. Thus esoteric knowledge is an experience which must remain for him alone who has had it, since it cannot be communicated, and exoteric knowledge is that which can be communicated, though we may decide that it is not desirable to do so. In that last case our exoteric knowledge is at the same time secret or hidden knowledge, and at some future time we may decide to publish it and make it available for all. But real esoteric knowledge can never be made exoteric ; since it is esoteric by its own nature, it is incapable of being expressed. As Lao Tze expresses it at the beginning of the Tao Teh King : ' The Tao which can be expressed is not the unchanging Tao ; the Name which can be named is not the unchanging Name.'

It is the unripe mind which, not realizing even how reality should be *approached*, plunges into an unhesitating answer where the truly philosophical mind would in reverence seek for Reality. Truly, ' fools rush in, where angels fear to tread,' and it makes the philosopher shrink with horror to see a mind which cannot yet think beyond the futilities of everyday life deal readily, definitely and conclusively with subjects of which he himself has only begun to realize the depth and the mystery. We suffer pain as if a sacrilege were done to that which is holy to us, when we see the illusion-bound intellects fingering with a crude complacency and in utter lack of understanding the sacred Mysteries which we ourselves would approach with holy awe. And when a system or doctrine is produced for which it is claimed that it has an answer for any problems life may offer, then truly do we know that what is offered is not the utterance of living truth but the lifeless structure of an imprisoned intellect. Life is not logical and life is not systematical ; it is not reasonable nor is it useful ; if it could be expressed in a logical system it would no longer be life but death. The mystery of life is not a problem to be solved, but a reality to be experienced, and this experience of the mystery of life is true Theosophy. This Theosophy can never be expressed in a system, nor has it an answer for the problems of life ; it is too great for that ; instead of condescending to answer questions and problems born of illusion it leads its devotees away from the unreality of a world-image into a world of Reality where they themselves *are* the truth they contemplate.

The greatness of a true and living philosophy of life is not that it answers the problems of life, but that it does *not* answer them ; did it answer them it would but show that it was born of illusion even as they are. Its greatness lies in the fact that it is able to *transcend* the problems and questions, which are rooted in illusion, and, in the experience of living reality, forget these futile playthings.

The man who has experienced truth returns from his experience in awe and reverence ; he is filled with the greatness of the mystery he has beheld, which is now part of his very being. When confronted by the unreal questions which have haunted philosophy and religion for so many centuries he does not descend to their level and fulfil their unsound demand by an equally unsound and empty satisfaction ; rather does he speak words of reality in the power of which the questions fade away and are destroyed. To the intellect, bound in illusion, it will ever seem that he evades the questions which it has asked ; it demands an answer corresponding point for point to these questions, made up though they are of the fabric of illusion. And when the true philosopher fails, or even refuses, to answer illusion by illusion, but waves aside the products of the unreal and speaks with the voice of reality, then the intellect in its blindness shrugs the shoulders and with a contemptuous smile turns away towards its own empty speculations.

The life of Gautama the Buddha yields many examples of this impossibility of giving a satisfactory answer to intellectual questions rooted in illusion. Many a time did his disciples seek to obtain from the Tathagata definite answers to their direct questions concerning ultimate problems, but never was his reply a direct answer to such questions, more often would he make three or four contradictory statements, leaving his disciples in the midst of their intellectual confusion and trying to show them the futility of their questions.

One of them, the venerable Malunkyaputta, complained to the Buddha, saying he would not lead the religious life under the Blessed One, unless he elucidated to him the great questions of life. The Buddha answered him, saying :

> Malunkyaputta, any one who should say, ' I will not lead the religious life under The Blessed One until The Blessed One shall elucidate to me either that the world is eternal, or that the world is not eternal . . . or that the saint neither exists nor does not exist after death '—that person would die, Malunkyaputta, before The Tathagata had ever elucidated this to him.
>
> It is as if, Malankyaputta, a man had been wounded by an arrow thickly smeared with poison, and his friends and companions, his relatives and kinsfolk, were to procure for him a physician or surgeon ; and the sick man were to say, ' I will not have this arrow taken out until I have learnt whether the man who wounded me belonged to the warrior caste, or to the Brahman caste, or to the agricultural caste, or to the menial caste.' That man would die, Malunkyaputta, without ever having learnt this.
>
> In exactly the same way, Malunkyaputta, any one who should say, ' I will not lead the religious life under The Blessed One until The Blessed One shall elucidate to me either that the

world is eternal, or that the world is not eternal . . . or that the saint neither exists nor does not exist after death '—that person would die, Malunkyaputta, before The Tathagata had ever elucidated this to him. (Warren, *Buddhism in Translations*, p. 117.)

Thus the Buddha refused to answer the questions born of illusion ; having attained to the full realization of truth he knew but too well that whatsoever answer he might give would be but partial truth and therefore misleading. He therefore abstained from giving direct answers, but showed his disciples the noble eightfold Path by which they themselves could conquer illusion and attain to reality. That is the cure for the poison of which he spoke to Malunkyaputta ; until we are thus cured no teaching can avail us, all we hear and know is poisoned by illusion.

It is significant to see how the very questions which the Buddha refrained from answering, well knowing the real answer to be impossible, are glibly answered by the immature intellect. To it the question and the answer are but as the mutually fitting pieces of a picture puzzle, and it is satisfied when the pieces fit. It has not even begun to realize something of the reality to which its questions pertain ; had it done so its questions would be very different or perhaps would not be asked at all, since it is a profound truth that when once we can really ask we also know. To ask in the real sense of the word is to aspire to the reality which alone can give satisfaction ; once we can ask in that way we are beginning to tread the path which leads to reality even though for the moment we may seem to ignore the questions which seem so vital to the intellect. The doctrine of the Buddha, teaching that man should first gain liberation from illusion, proves ultimately the shortest way to the realization of truth. ' Seek ye first the Kingdom of God and his righteousness and all these things shall be added unto you.'

CHAPTER FIVE

THE MYSTERY OF CREATION

*This universe, the same for all, no one, either god or man, has made ;
but it always was, and is, and ever shall be an ever-living fire,
fixed measures kindling and fixed measures dying out.*—HERACLITUS.

THE PROBLEM OF ORIGINS

IT is inevitable that man, contemplating his world-image and
assuming it to be an objective universe, should ask what the
origin of that world is, who made it and out of what it was
formed. In his daily experience all the objects he sees are
made somehow, they have a maker and are made out of some
material, there was a time when they were not, there was a
time when they became what they are now and there will be
a time when they shall no longer be what they are at present.
It is the same with regard to forms in nature ; he sees them
grow from small beginnings to maturity and finally decay or
disintegrate. Transferring these experiences to the universe
surrounding him, man wonders how this universe began ;
whether there was anything before it and whether some day
it will come to an end ; whether it grew by itself to be what it
is now or whether it had a Maker who created it ; whether
this Creator made his universe out of some pre-existing
material or whether he, somehow, evolved it out of himself ;
what the present relation of this universe is to its first Cause,
what the end of it will be and whether there is a purpose
in its existence and growth.

Many and various are the answers which man gives to
these questions of world-origins, from the crude versions of

primitive mythology to the mature theological views in which
an extra-cosmic Deity makes the world out of nothing, or the
scientific conception of a mechanical evolution in which this
world in all its complexity emerges by itself from a stellar
nebula. And in most great philosophies we find some contribution to these problems of world-creation, some attempt
to explain the mystery. Thus from the earliest periods of
Hindu philosophy down to the most modern philosophical
theories the problems connected with the origin of this
universe have thrust themselves into man's contemplation
with a persistence that will not be denied.

The more primitive the race or civilization the more naive
its solution of the questions of creation ; reading some of
these ancient explanations we may well wonder that they were
ever taken seriously. We feel that our age has entirely outgrown such childish fabulations, and yet, when we come to
analyze the attitude of the average man with regard to these
problems, it is surprising to see how exceedingly primitive
his very approach to the question is. Thus we still find many
millions of Christians, a number of whom have had the
advantage of a scientific training, accepting unquestioningly
as God's word the primitive tradition which the Jewish nation
held to account for the origin of man and the universe.

It was the primitive anthropomorphism and the inherent
contradictions of the story of Genesis which made Shelley
write in Queen Mab :

> From an eternity of idleness
> I, God, awoke ; in seven days toil made earth
> From nothing ; rested, and created man.
> I placed him in a paradise and there
> Planted the tree of evil, so that he
> Might eat and perish and my soul procure
> Wherewith to sate its malice and to turn
> Even like a heartless conqueror of the earth
> All misery to my fame.

And yet Shelley's was an essentially religious nature : it was the very depth of his religious realization which made him put aside a primitive tradition which, with all its discrepancies, can hardly be taken to be God's word without a serious reflection on His omniscience.

There is no doubt but that the Old Testament is one of the most precious parts of the world's literature. As a history of the struggles and aspirations of a most interesting and gifted nation, as a tradition of their religious thoughts and feelings, as a document of human weakness and strength, of beauty and brutality, it has perhaps no equal in the literature of any country. As such it will always yield plentiful fruits to those who study it and it will always widen our human understanding and outlook. But to accept every word of that Scripture as not only divinely inspired, but as God's own word, is an absurdity which should be incompatible with modern thought.

We must not underestimate the influence which even to-day the Old Testament has on Christian mentality ; many of its conceptions concerning God and the world, man and woman, evil and sin, have, through many centuries of Christian tradition, been woven into the very texture of our thoughts, unconscious though we may be of the fact.

THE SCIENTIFIC ANSWER

It is but natural that those who turn away from a version of world creation which offends the thinking mind at every point, should look towards science to give a reasonable explanation of world-origins. In fact, it was largely because of the discoveries of science in the domains of astronomy, geology, palaeontology and archaeology that the first shadow of doubt was cast on biblical accuracy, and soon the choice became that of accepting either the version of Genesis

concerning the creation of our world, or else the data of
science with the theories based on them.

Since the geologist knows approximately the rate of
geological deposit he can, when studying the strata of the
earth's surface judge with comparative exactness the age of
any particular layer. If, therefore, he finds that certain layers
are a hundred thousand or many hundreds of thousands of
years old, and if in such layers are found remains either of
human beings, or of extinct animals or plants, such remains
bear a mute witness to the existence of the creatures in
question at that period. There is no doubt that the testimony
of these geological deposits is contradictory not only to the
Mosaic chronology, but also to the succession of natural
species as presented in Genesis. Instead of a number of
spontaneous creations by an extra-cosmic Deity we find a
gradual process of change in which a new species by very
slow and gradual changes grows from previous ones. Thus
man, instead of being created completely and perfectly by
God, is considered to be the natural descendant of ape-like
ancestors ; Genesis and science appear incompatible.

In this earlier conception of the evolution of species the
method, by which a new species was thought to have emerged
from previous ones, was that of adaptation to environment
and natural selection by a survival of the fittest. For a
creative intelligence there was no place in this classical
theory of evolution ; the task of the God of Moses had been
taken over by a new God whose name was ' adaptation to
environment.' We can but wonder that many a free thinker,
who rejected contemptuously the miraculous creation of the
world as taught in Genesis, willingly accepted the no less
miraculous evolution of the world, with all its variety of
creatures, from a stellar nebula by the miraculous agencies
called adaptation to environment and survival of the fittest.

Truly, when we are asked to believe that our modern world with its millions of different creatures, with the marvellous complexity of structure in the animal and vegetable kingdoms, with man himself in the strength of his aspirations and his power to adapt environment to himself, that all this should have grown from the stellar nebula by adaptation and survival, we must acknowledge that we are face to face with a miracle compared to which that of Genesis is but child's play.

But apart from the miracle demanded by the older evolutionists there are serious insufficiencies in their conception. None can doubt the influence of environment and the truth of the survival of the fittest, but on the other hand it is equally true that it was not always the fittest who survived. When the flying creature gradually evolved from the reptile there must have been a period stretching perhaps through thousands of years when the rudimentary wings were not sufficiently perfect to allow for their use in flying and during which, consequently, the creature with evolving wings would be inferior instead of superior to its fellow reptiles. Neither adaptation to environment nor survival of the fittest by natural selection can ever explain how the bird-like creature evolved from the reptile, since only the fully evolved wing would give its possessor superiority over creatures without wings. Thus we cannot escape the conclusion that there must be a force within the species which causes it to evolve into the higher one and to survive in an intervening period when, by reason of its changing structure, it is temporarily inferior instead of superior to its mates. This indwelling, formative principle, the creative life-urge or *élan vital*, becomes then the cause of evolution, in which environment and the struggle for life are *utilized* to accomplish a purpose which, by themselves, they could never achieve.

It becomes, then, the function which determines the organ,

there is an evolution of life which, from within, determines
the evolution of form and creates the new species by the force
of an indwelling, dynamic principle which, if we are to judge
by results, must be intelligent. We might as well believe
that a heap of bricks could form themselves into a beautiful
building without the influence of a creative intelligence as
believe that the beauty of form in Nature has evolved out of
the matter of the stellar nebula by the chance of natural
selection.

The science of evolution, then, recalls, under another form
and name, the Creator whom it expelled in its earlier stages
and, where previously religion and science were opponents,
we can now see the possibility of a synthesis of the two in a
higher truth. This does not mean, of course, that the
incompatibilities of Genesis with modern science will ever
be overcome, but it does mean that the data of science are
not in any way incompatible with the belief in a creative
Intelligence, directing and guiding evolution from within.

THE INSUFFICIENCY OF THE SCIENTIFIC ANSWER

Illuminating and indispensable as evolution is in explaining
the method by which change takes place in our universe, it
is yet, like all scientific truth, an explanation of the *how*, not
of the *why* ; the method is explained, the mystery is not
touched at all. Even if we do trace this universe back to
stellar nebula the question remains, whence the nebula
and if that nebula in turn is supposed to have emerged from
some primordial matter the question yet remains, whence
this primordial matter, and why did it change into the nebula ?
We are still confronted by an ultimate matter, a raw material
out of which the universe has been evolved, but which in
itself remains unexplained. Equally unexplained remains
the differentiation of a varied universe out of the supposed

uniformity of a primordial substance. And above all there remains the question of the indwelling creative power which causes primitive forms to evolve into ever higher ones. Evolution too is incapable of finding a true beginning, it too fails to co-ordinate our universe of time and change with an eternal, abiding Reality. Thus Taylor, in his contribution to *Evolution in the light of modern knowledge*, says :

> Hence there can be no final ' evolutionary ' explanation of being as a whole, any more than there can be a manufacture of manifold and different objects out of a ' raw material ' which has no character of its own and is thus pure nothing. Every evolution presupposes both a material and agencies acting on the material which are anterior to the evolution itself, and the process of accounting for these *praesupposita* as the results of a still earlier evolution cannot ' go to infinity.' Somewhere behind all evolutions and supplying all with ' material ' and ' driving force ' there must be the strictly eternal.

However illuminating the discoveries of science are and have been with regard to natural evolution, the mystery of creation is not even touched by them. Science can never find an ultimate creative Agency, nor a true origin of things ; it can but trace its origins back to previous evolutions, universes or structures, the *praesupposita* of which Taylor speaks, and these are left unexplained.

The same insufficiencies which we meet in the scientific view of world-origins present themselves when we enter the realm of occultism, which, as explained before, should be considered as an extension of science into worlds of subtler matter. On the basis of clairvoyant investigation certain facts are put forward which trace the creative process to a point beyond that which ordinary science can reach. Thus, in modern theosophy, we find a doctrine of creation, in which the Logos of a solar system is presented as creating His solar system by pouring forth His power into a pre-existing Root of matter termed *Mulaprakriti*, thus causing the formation of primordial atoms. The arising of differentiation out of the apparent nothingness of unmanifest Being is explained by the connection of one cycle of manifestation or *manvantara* with a previous one, the two being separated in time by a period called *pralaya* or non-manifestation, during which the fruits of the previous manvantara are kept in abeyance until the beginning of the next manvantara when they re-emerge and cause the differentiation of the One into the Many.

These doctrines, based on occult investigation, offer an interesting extension of science beyond the physical, but they do not even touch the mystery of creation itself. To trace the origin of matter to a pre-existent root of matter does not explain the fundamental problem of origins any more than the theological doctrine of the creation of the universe out of nothing ; we have merely shifted the problem. In the same way the question of the beginning of creation is not touched by shifting back that beginning one or even one thousand manvantaras, even if each of these should last three hundred times a million years. Such enormous numbers may dazzle the imagination ; to the problem of time and the eternal they contribute no solution.

This does not in the least impair the value of the occult doctrines concerning creation and the origin of matter, but the remarks of Taylor with regard to the philosophical insufficiency of the scientific theories still hold good ; we start from *praesupposita* as the results of an earlier evolution and we are still confronted by the impossibility of finding a beginning. Occultism necessarily shares the fate of science in the face of ultimate questions ; it too can explain method, the how, but never the why.

WRONG QUESTIONS AND WRONG ANSWERS

The fundamental reason why neither the theological nor the scientific or even the occult view of world-origins can ever give a satisfactory answer is that they all begin by implicitly accepting the questions, without pausing to consider whether perhaps something is not wrong with the question itself, and whether we do not stand self-condemned when we attempt to answer it.

As long as the intellect does not even suspect that its objective universe is but the world-image produced in our consciousness it will unquestioningly accept an absolute time as part of that objective universe. Such an objective time demands beginning and end, and the intellect finds itself confronted by this difficulty that creation must have begun at some time, that is to say, that there must have been a beginning of time. This is in itself absurd, especially when thought of in conjunction with an unchanging eternity of divine existence. It is impossible to co-ordinate our cycles of time, or definite duration, with an unchanging eternity which has neither beginning nor end, being an ever present reality, and all our attempts to make our illusion of an absolute time fit in with the conception of eternity are doomed to failure.

In a similar way the intellect finds itself in an *impasse* when it tries to understand how, on the one hand, there must have been something out of which the universe was made and on the other hand that something itself must have been made somehow and can hardly have an objective existence outside the One who made it. Yet creation out of nothing is but a phrase, and not even the more immaterial conceptions of emanation from God's being or existence in God's thought can shed light on the final mystery. All such terms may be applied to the work of the Deity of a universe with regard to His especial system, where we are in the realm of relativity and can use terms derived therefrom. But when we are trying to approach the ultimate mystery of creation we must go by a different path altogether and first overcome the illusion out of which our erroneous questions are born.

Naturally, as long as we believe our world-image to be an objective universe, independent of our consciousness, we are confronted by the problem of the objective materiality of that universe, and all our questions concerning creation presuppose such an entirely real and objective matter. Our questions and answers are thus born of illusion and until we, in ourselves, conquer that illusion it is impossible to approach the mystery of creation at all. As long as we are subject to preconceived ideas, rooted in illusion, colouring all our questions, it is better for us not to ask anything at all ; we are but as the man wounded by the poisoned arrow in the story of Malunkyaputta, what we first need is the physician. Until we gain experience of reality the best we can do is to make ingenious explanations of impossible situations, for such are our questions and answers as long as we are in the throes of illusion. They may satisfy us for a while by their very ingenuity, but they are empty of meaning.

Thus in all the questions concerning the first Cause, the beginning of creation, the matter out of which the universe is made, its origin and the relation of our universe to its Creator, illusions enter, especially the illusions of an absolute time and of the objective reality of matter, and the questions can never be solved, being wrong in themselves. Yet the very intensity of our desire to know, our very passion for truth in these matters and the sincerity and whole-heartedness with which we have asked the questions, however wrong these may be, provide the motive power which finally must bring us to reality. Even in wrong questions there is virtue according to the measure of their sincerity and whole-heartedness.

It is useless, as we have seen, to ask of science an answer to ultimate questions concerning creation ; science may explain to us how things work in our world-image and how, in the *circulus vitiosus* of time, one thing is connected with others in a seemingly endless chain of causation ; ultimate questions fall outside its domain. It is the same with occultism ; on the basis of clairvoyant investigation certain facts may be put forward which trace the creative process to a point beyond that which ordinary science can reach. But all this, profoundly interesting and valuable as it may be in explaining the methods of growth and of change as seen in our world-image, does not contribute anything essential to the philosophical problems with regard to world origins. Science and occultism, belonging as they do to the domain of the relative, contribute but facts, and to present their findings as philosophical answers is but to misapply them. The mystery of creation must be approached in a different way altogether ; having stated our problem as clearly as we can we must surrender our world-image and all that belongs to it and, in the world of the Real, try to experience the Mystery itself.

TIME AND THE ETERNAL

Let us then withdraw from our world-image with its compelling illusions and enter that world of Reality, where alone living truth can be experienced.

Here we have left behind us the world of relativity, we are the Absolute which is all relativity simultaneously and eternally. No longer do we now gaze upon a universe, the history of which enrolls itself in time ; we experience as an ever-present reality That which, speaking our language of illusion, is all that is, was or shall be, all universe past and present, all beginnings and endings, all cycles of time and evolution. Yet the Absolute is not on one side and all the manifoldness of relativity on the other. Relativity is but the spelling of the Name of the Absolute, it is its very being, its constitution, its description, we might almost say its one characteristic. That is why in the experience of Reality it seems absurd to ask how the relative originated in the Absolute, whence it came and why it is ; it *is* the Absolute and is only seen as the relative when viewed from the relative standpoint of some creature in its illusion of separateness.

It is therefore impossible to say that there is some reason for the presence of the relative in the Absolute, it is not ' present in ' the Absolute, it is but the Absolute, experienced in a different way. Thus there is no *raison d'être* for the relative, no origin or cause of it, it has no purpose and serves no end and in no way does it increase the glory of the Absolute, since it is the Absolute. Words like origin and cause, purpose and end can only flower in the soil of illusion, they lose their meaning in the world of the Real.

Of the relative as well as of the Absolute we can but say that its being is its justification, it is and it is all there is, it always was and never shall cease to be, though ' never ' and ' always ' are again terms derived from our language of illusion. Ever-present reality is the mystery we experience in the world of the Real and in that experience questions cease.

It is here that the intellect must always labour under misconceptions, to it the ever-present Reality of all that is can but appear as a frozen immobility ; the silence and changelessness of the Eternal is to the intellect but as the stillness of death. To it life is movement and movement means change, one thing *after* another. And yet the experience of the Real is far from that which the intellect would picture it to be ; though the Eternal is changeless, all change and time, growth and evolution are contained in it as an abiding reality, whereas in our world-image we see them unrolled on the endless scroll we call time. What we experience in our time consciousness is but the ever-shifting section of reality which we term the present.

The present in itself has neither duration nor reality ; not even the fraction of a second can be called the present. Only past and future are real and are the names we give to the ever-present reality of things as they are. It is therefore as impossible to speak of the beginning or end of anything in the world of the Real as it is to speak of the beginning or end of a circle. Beginning and end, growth and change, successive stages only appear when, in our world-image, we interpret ever-present Reality.

An image may help us to realize something of that which is of necessity beyond the intellect. If we imagine a being living in a two-dimensional world, for instance the surface of a liquid, we can readily see how any object passed through the surface of that liquid would present to the two-dimensional being an ever-changing cross-section of its true being. That ever-shifting cross-section would be the only experience the two-dimensional being had of the three-dimensional reality. If we passed a cone through its two-dimensional surface it might first see the point of contact of the extreme end of the cone and then an ever-widening circle or ellipse according to the angle at which the cone was passed through its two-dimensional world. We can imagine how this two-dimensional creature might give the name ' cone ' to that cross-section of the cone, which is all it knows, and might view the constant change of that cross-section as the ' evolution ' of the cone from a point into a large circle. Yet, that which would appear as change or evolution to the two-dimensional being would be a simultaneously present reality to a three-dimensional being looking on ; to it the cone would be one complete thing. Again the surface creature would call ' past ' that which had passed through its surface and ' future ' that which had not yet passed through, whereas its ' present ' would be the ever-changing cross-section. To the three-dimensional onlooker that present would have no substance; the past and future would make up the real being.

Thus each relative being in the world of the Real is simultaneously all that which, in the time-illusion of our world-image, we call its history or evolution. While in that illusion of time we do but see ever-shifting cross-sections of eternal Reality, in the world of the Real every being is complete, containing in itself its entire evolution as a simultaneously present reality. Our particular cycle of evolution with apparent beginning and end is but *our* realization·in time of that which we are in eternity. That which we realize in our cycle of life, in the world of time, is real enough, it is our eternal being, but the *way* we realize it as a process of growth, with beginning and end, that is our idiosyncrasy, our illusion.

Every creature has its realization of eternal reality and that realization is the life-cycle of that creature. Our life-cycle as a whole is our being in the world of the Real, seen as our evolution in the illusion of the world-image. Thus what we call our evolution as an individual is like the spelling, letter for letter, of our eternal Name, our true being ; as such it seems to accomplish a purpose, to lead to some end, to produce some result and to have a cause, whereas all these words seem meaningless when thought of in connection with the reality that produces the appearance of evolution in our world-image.

In a similar way our activity, or rather that which we hold to be our activity, is our realization of the eternal Activity, the only Activity which ever exists—the Rhythm of creation. In our daily consciousness we may be intensely aware that we do things, think thoughts and feel emotions, they form our activity, our work or creation, emerging from us, done by us. When we make a table or speak a word we feel that we are creating something which, in that form, did not exist before, we feel that we are, all the time, adding something to the totality of things. In a similar way, but on an infinitely larger scale, we think of the Deity of a universe as creating that universe, making or thinking it, or even emanating it out of Himself, but always adding by His activity to the sum total of things at that moment. Yet, once again, this is but illusion.

There is nothing, there never was anything, there never can be anything but the eternal Rhythm of creation, unchanging, containing all things. It is the Absolute, It is at the same time all relativity all that we think of as past, present or future. It is all universes with their uncounted millions of creatures and objects, it is in eternal and abiding reality all that we think of as their actions or creations. What we call the activity of a relative being, however lofty, is its realization in the realm of relativity of the eternal Rhythm of creation. That realization by the separate creature appears to have beginning and end, it appears to be the individual and unique creation of that being, but in reality it is only its realization of eternal Creation. That realization is unique in so far as it is the realization of that particular being or creature, yet the thought that the separate creature produces its creation, adds it as it were to the general store, is illusion.

Whenever, in our world-image, we search for origins, by means of science or occultism, we are always searching for origins of a particular universe, however great, in the realm of relativity. The reason why it will always be impossible to find these origins or to find an end is that such a universe *is not the objective creation we think it to be, but the realization by some great Being of eternal Creation.* The apparent beginning and end of that creation are only relative to the Being whose realization that universe is ; we cannot find an objective beginning or end because there is none. What we call time is but a linear interpretation of the circle of eternal Being, its beginning and end, however loudly clamoured for, can never be found. Thus our individual cycle of time, our evolution, is our experience of eternal Reality within the greater cycle of time which is the experience of reality by the indwelling Life of our universe, but none of these cycles of time are objectively real, they are experiences of Reality.

THE RHYTHM OF CREATION

On the one hand, in our normal consciousness, we can experience the fact of the limitation of the Absolute in the relative ; on the other hand, in our experience of reality, we find the fact of the liberation of the relative into the Absolute. These two *facts*—the eternal limitation of the Absolute to the relative and the eternal liberation of the relative into the Absolute are not merely the fruits of intellectual reasoning or of logical proof, they are realities which we can experience *in ourselves*. Together these two basic facts interpret for us the mystery of Creation ; deceptive as the terms limitation and liberation are in their insufficiency they serve to describe for us the eternal Creation which is the being of the Absolute. Together they express the Rhythm of Creation.

When we enter the world of the Real we not only experience the liberation from relative to Absolute, we become the eternal creative Rhythm which is the very Being of the Absolute, which is the Absolute itself. In that ultimate experience there is no longer question of two basic facts of consciousness which together yield the creative Rhythm; we experience the Rhythm of creation as the supreme and final Reality, beyond which nothing is and which is all things. In the experience of that Rhythm we can recognize the phases of limitation and liberation, but they are *our* distinctions, not in any way separations in the creative Rhythm. That Rhythm is *one and whole ;* in it the limitation of the Absolute as relativity and the liberation of the relative in the Absolute are a simultaneous, all-pervading, ultimate Reality.

It is true, even the term ' rhythm ' is insufficient, but, when we have experienced reality, we find ourselves placed before this choice—either to say nothing at all, recognizing that no words can express the Real, or else to attempt to convey something of reality in a language based on our world-image illusions, well knowing that *everyone of our expressions must be insufficient and thereby misleading*, and that whatever we say must appear to be self-contradictory. This is why the use of symbols is such a great help ; in a symbol we can express simultaneously that which in language we can only describe as a sequence. Yet we must not forget that, since in the language of symbolism we use measures of space, the illusions inherent to an objective space are as great a danger in our symbols as the illusions inherent in an objective time are in our language of words.

In the symbol of the circle we can realize as a simultaneous reality the Rhythm of creation which, when described in language, must ever appear to be a sequence of one thing after another. Especially when we can see the circle as radiation, and not as a combination of centre and circumference, it is a great help towards the understanding of that which is beyond understanding. In this symbol the limitation of Absolute to relative is seen in the movement from the centre, the liberation of the relative into the Absolute in the movement back toward the centre.

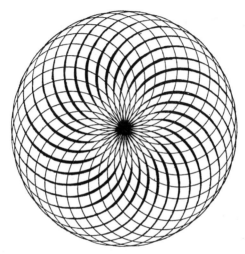

DIAGRAM THREE—The circle as symbol of the creative Rhythm.

In the experience of reality there is, of course, no question of a going forth or a coming back, but the nearest description we can give of the eternal Rhythm of creation is that of a twofold process—an eternal going forth from the unity of all-comprehensive reality to the uttermost differentiation in relativity and an eternal return from that realm of relativity towards the centre in which the whole is simultaneously realized. It is the eternal Tide of creation, the ebb and flow of all things, not successive but simultaneous or rather eternal; it is the eternal Heart-beat with its diastole and systole, the eternal Breath of creation which yet is an unchanging reality.

The experience of the Rhythm of creation is the ultimate experience in the quest of Truth. To say that it is great or glorious, wonderful or all-surpassing, is but to belittle it, it cannot be compared to anything since it is all things and there is naught beyond it ; it is without cause or purpose. It is the Song of the Eternal of which all things, great or small, form part, all being notes and chords in an eternal Harmony which is ultimate Being. When once we have entered the world of Reality and *been* the Rhythm of creation we know it in all things ; every object, every creature, every event now has for us its true significance as a note in the Symphony of creation. All things join in that eternal Song ; nothing now exists for us except as part of the Song of creation. By itself a thing seems absurd and without meaning as a single note would be ; we now realize that indeed there is no such thing as a separate note in the Song or creation but only the one comprehensive Reality in which is infinite variety, but no separateness.

In mystical philosophy this remains the supreme experience which yet is more than an experience, since we *are* that which we know, and in that being are no longer ourselves, but That which is all things. In the realization of the Rhythm of creation all else becomes clear to us, henceforth we see things in the light of the Eternal, we behold them *sub specie aeternitatis ;* in the nameless Reality we know the names of all things.

THE ABSOLUTE AS CREATION

The Absolute does not create, it *is* eternal creation ; creation is its Being, its Name, its Nature, not even co-eternal with It, since it is not distinct from It. That is the ultimate mystery which has neither cause nor purpose.

The very word creation, however, is misleading, it at once

brings in its train mental associations of a Creator who creates something—the creature. All such terms are the product of the externalization of our world-image as objective reality ; in the illusion of our daily contemplation of that world-image we produce the construction maker, making, thing made— and this construction we transfer to the ultimate question of creation. Thus the very word ' creation,' which means but ' making,' is the product of our illusion and we must be careful in using the term in connection with ultimate Reality.

In that Reality there is no dual structure ; all duality is rooted in the illusion which results when we externalize our world-image and consider it to be an objective reality, separate from our consciousness. Then we posit a self within and a not-self without, spirit or life within, matter or form without, and we look upon our life as an interplay between the two. We then transfer this dual structure, born of illusion, into our metaphysical speculations and look upon the mystery of creation as an act, thought or event, whereby something, the objective universe, emerges out of something else. Thus even the more subtle theories of the universe as a divine Emanation, or even as the thought or imagination of God, harbour conceptions, which belong to the world of relativity and are justified there, but which have no place or meaning in the world of the Absolute.

It is curious to see how, in the philosophy of Hinduism, as well as in several Western philosophies we find the construction of Self—Not-Self, which is a product of our daily illusion, transferred to ultimate realities.

Nothing is in itself either self or not-self, these are but relative terms arising from our daily experience, and the same thing or being which, in that experience, is realized as not-self may well be self with regard to something else. Thus it is empty of meaning to speak of a universal Self and a universal Not-Self, there are no such ultimates, they are abstractions from our daily experience.

But even if we drop these misleading terms 'self' and 'not-self' and speak of the One and the Many, or even the Absolute and the relative, we can never explain creation as an interplay between these two opposites. Absolute and relative are not a duality of opposites between which the Web of Life is spun, creation is not a divine ferry-service which goes from the One to the Many and then back again to the One. It is true, in the eternal 'process' of creation we can certainly distinguish a stage where the Absolute is oblivious of itself in the limitation of the relative and the separate creature knows itself but as one among many. We can experience this stage in ourselves in our ordinary daily consciousness where we feel ourselves to be the separate creature and see around us a world of manifoldness. On the other hand, in our realization of the Absolute, we know ourselves to be that which is all things in unchanging unity. Yet we cannot say that creation is the going from the one stage to the other and back again. If we, in our contemplation of reality, distinguish in it certain periods or stages these may be a mental convenience to us, but we cannot assign objective reality to them.

In the swing of a pendulum we can distinguish the moment of its highest elevation sideways and the moment where it reaches the neutral position in the centre, through which again it will swing to the highest elevation on the other side. We can, however, not characterize the swing of the pendulum as a connection between those different moments of its movement, rather should we say that these moments are but phases which we distinguish in the swinging movement as such. The swinging movement is the fundamental reality, any stages we desire to distinguish in it are mental conveni-

ences to us, not realities. In the same way creation is the
fundamental reality and any stages we wish to distinguish in
it may be convenient to us in our attempts to comprehend
intellectually something of a reality which is beyond our
intellect, but they must not be taken as objective realities ;
they denote a relation and nothing more.

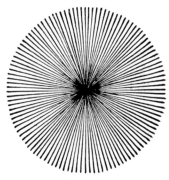

DIAGRAM FOUR.—The circle as radiation from a point.

If once again we contemplate the symbol of the circle we
may find it easier to approach the reality. In the circle again
we can distinguish centre and circumference which to us may
symbolize respectively the One and the Many. We may
think of rays in that circle as connections between centre and
circumference, and we can draw them as such by moving our
pencil from the centre to the circumference or back again to
the centre. Yet we should make a great mistake if we
therefore characterized radiation as a connection between the
centre of a circle and its circumference. Radiation remains
the fundamental reality of a circle and in that radiation the
point from which it takes place gains the significance of
centre and the limit to which it goes gains the meaning of
circumference. Centre and circumference are thus but

periods or stages, moments which we distinguish in the process of radiation ; no radiation no circle and consequently no centre or circumference.

There is but one Reality which we may term the Absolute or the Relative, the very being of which is eternal Creation or eternal Becoming. If in that eternal creative Rhythm we distinguish one phase in which the relative is oblivious of the Absolute, seeing but separateness and an external universe of relativity, and another phase in which the relative once again realizes itself as the Absolute and in that realization *is* the Absolute, even so these phases are but distinctions *we* make in that which is entire and whole—the one, ultimate eternal Reality.

When, in the world of the Real, we realize the ultimate reality of the Absolute as creation or eternal becoming, when we know the Rhythm of creation as the very being of the Absolute, we can see the absurdity of those questions which ask out of what material the universe is made, who made it and how it was made. All these questions originate in illusion, and, unless we conquer this illusion in ourselves from the beginning, we shall find it coming up in subtle forms at every step of our philosophical contemplations.

To the intellect in its limitation the realization which we gain of the Absolute as creation is very unsatisfactory, since it does not in any way solve or explain the problems which the intellect constructed and for the answer of which it clamours. But when we gain the experience of this ultimate Reality we find the questions disappearing in the light of Reality ; in that light we can see the absurdity and distortion inherent in the questions and problems which the intellect considers so seriously and so strenuously. We do not in any way solve the problem of creation, we experience the reality in which the problem is seen as the product of illusion.

In that ultimate experience we know that the Absolute is eternal creation, that creation is not an act, thought or emanation of the Absolute but that it *is* the Absolute, its very being, ultimate reality, causeless, without beginning, end or purpose. It is the one Reality beyond which nothing is, there is no cause to which the one eternal truth can be traced, no final result which it can ever produce or accomplish. We may call this ultimate reality the Absolute or the relative, the two terms refer to the same Reality, which is the relative when experienced by the separate creature as a world of separateness and multiplicity, which is the Absolute when realized as That which is all relativity, past and future, in ever-present Reality. That Reality is Creation, it is the final and awful Truth which we realize in the world of eternal reality the 'one dark truth' of which Dionysius speaks. Truly this final mystery is awful and dark, yet its darkness is better than the light of our world-image and the awe with which it fills us is better than the self-complacent conceit of the intellect. It leaves us silent, for its simplicity is too great to be expressed. It is a mystery, the Mystery of Creation, the ultimate Mystery, but it is no longer a problem since we ourselves are It.

CHAPTER SIX

SPIRIT AND MATTER

The nature of these revelations is the same ; they are perceptions of the absolute law. They are solutions of the soul's own questions. They do not answer the questions which the understanding asks. The soul answers never by words, but by the thing itself that is inquired after.—EMERSON, *The Over-Soul.*

THE PROBLEM OF DUALITY

THE antithesis of a solid, tangible and visible world around us and an invisible, intangible and subtle consciousness or life within is so fundamentally the structure of our world and so utterly permeates our outlook on life that it hardly occurs to us to analyze or doubt it. We unthinkingly accept the two terms of that duality as really opposed and ask ourselves whence the duality arises, how its two elements are related and how one can affect the other.

The names given to the opposites in this duality of our daily experience vary ; they may be termed spirit and matter, life and form, self and not-self, energy and mass, but fundamentally they are that duality which appears to be the main structure of our lives. In ourselves we are sharply aware of the two opposites as body and mind ; our life appears to be sensation, coming to us from without, the body affecting the mind, and on the other hand action and volition, coming from within, the mind affecting the body. Instinctively we recognize the difference, whatever philosophical theory we may cherish, we cannot escape from the fact that to us this interaction between mind and body, between world within and world without, is a daily reality. Even the philosopher, who in his speculations should attempt to deny the fact of this duality altogether, will find himself painfully reminded of it each time the law of his members wars against the law of his spirit, when he does that which he does not want to do or does not do that which he wants to do. Each time we experience the struggle between the body and its desires and the mind with its decisions the duality of our lives is brought home to us, and no theory can reason away that experience.

In mechanics and physics we are confronted by the same fundamental duality in the terms of energy and mass. We know but too well that, when we wish to lift a heavy weight, energy or force is needed and the distinction between the inert, heavy and solid mass we desire to move and the intangible, invisible energy we use to move it is sharp and undeniable. In fact, we might say that there is not an experience in our daily lives which does not show this dual construction in some form or other. The consciousness we have of ourselves as being a self, the way in which we look upon all else as being not-self, permeates our very lives, is manifest in every one of our experiences.

It is therefore but natural that the relation between body and mind, or matter and spirit, should be the fundamental problem of philosophy, the most prolific of all philosophical questions ; there is hardly a philosophy which has not some contribution to offer towards this true riddle of the sphinx— a divine head on an animal body.

To find an explanation of this most outstanding problem of our daily life is a necessity ; all day long we are aware of mind acting on body and body acting on mind, of energy moving mass and mass resisting energy and, if we are at all awake to the wonder and mystery of life, we must feel an eagerness, an intense desire to know how this interaction takes place. Even if, later on, we are to find that there are serious flaws in the problem itself, even though we may find that the problem as it stands cannot be solved, yet the desire to know and the intensity with which we demand an answer are of the greatest value. It is only according to the intensity of our questions that our ultimate experience of truth will be. If we ask our philosophical questions in a casual and indifferent way, in the attitude ' that it would be interesting to know these things,' we shall certainly never emerge beyond a superficial intellectualism. Almost every one of us occasionally does ask some philosophical question of the profoundest meaning—the purpose of life, the origin of the world, the ultimate reality of spirit or matter or the measure of freedom of the human will. But in most cases the one who asks lives on quite happily, even though he may not find an answer or experience the reality. Such is not the way of true philosophy ; unless we ask with our whole being, heart and soul and mind, unless we can hardly eat or drink or sleep unless we know, unless life is no longer worth living without the experience of living truth, we shall not gain it. We must desire truth more than life itself if we are to be worthy of experiencing it.

Read but in the *Confessions* how St. Augustine yearned for truth ; he speaks of his ' most ardent pursuit of truth and wisdom,' says that he is ' struggling for the breath of Thy truth,' and exclaims when he questions the nature of time :

My soul is all on fire to be resolved of this most intricate difficulty. Shut it not up, O Lord God, O my good Father ; in the name of Christ, I beseech thee, do not so shut up these usual, but yet hidden things, from this desire of mine, that it be hindered from piercing into them : and let them shine out unto me, thy mercy, O Lord, enlightening me.

And again, when he contemplates the problem of evil, he speaks of the ' torment which his teeming heart endured,' saying that ' no man knew how much he suffered.' Such is the attitude of the seeker after truth and such are they who find ; as long, however, as the problem is to us but an intellectual puzzle to be solved as well as possible, so long shall our answers but be ingenious explanations and nothing more.

According to the type or mentality of a philosopher or of some particular period will be the answer given to the fundamental problem of duality ; unknown to himself the philosopher will be influenced in his logical and well-reasoned theory by his own spontaneous attitude towards this dual universe. It would be of interest if, some day, a history of philosophy could be written in which the philosophical doctrines held by the leading philosophers were to be shown as the inevitable product of their own innate tendencies, desires and difficulties, rather than of their profound reasoning and irrefutable logic. It is often our general outlook on life, the way we feel towards the world surrounding us and towards our fellow men, our aspirations and struggles, our achievements and failures, which determine our philosophy and its doctrines, not these doctrines which determine our outlook on life. We accept or evolve a philosophy of life because it provides a framework within which our spontaneous tendencies can work, even though we may feel convinced that we have been won over to them by the logic of their propositions and the strength of their proof. It would not be difficult to show how a Spinoza, Kant, Schopenhauer or Nietzsche was determined in his philosophical doctrines by virtue of that which he was rather than that which he thought out. St. Augustine's emphasis of original sin is as much the inevitable outcome of the incessant struggle which his passionate nature caused him, as Schopenhauer's pessimism was the result of his unhappy experiences and failures, reacting on a mind that could not rise triumphantly over them and gain strength instead of cynicism out of them. Had Schopenhauer been happy in his first love he would never have written his scathing words about women, had St. Augustine succeeded in harmonizing his passions with his religious aspirations he would never have condemned the unbaptized infant to everlasting hell. It is our outlook that causes our philosophy not our philosophy which causes our outlook.

There is therefore an element of truth and reality in everyone of the more serious approaches to the problem of our dual universe. In an unsympathetic discussion and criticism of philosophical doctrine it is no doubt always possible to present them in such a way that they appear but as the futile fantasies of arid minds, but if we try to understand a doctrine from the mentality of the one who produced it we shall always see that for that mentality and from that standpoint the doctrine was relatively true.

MONISTIC SOLUTIONS

It is impossible to imagine that mind can influence body or body influence mind, energy act on mass or mass on energy, unless there is something which unites the two terms in a higher unity or reduces them to one. If matter and spirit, body and mind were a real duality, each being essentially and fundamentally different from the other, it would be unthinkable, not only that they should influence one another, but even in any way be aware of one another's existence. Since their interaction is a fact in our universe we must come to the conclusion that they are not true opposites, entirely different one from another, having nothing in common, but that there must be a unity underlying them somehow ; our dual universe must be seen as a monistic universe, however we achieve that monism.

The most obvious ways of overcoming the dualism in our universe is to acknowledge only one of its two terms as real and to look upon the other as secondary, produced in some way by the first. Thus the materialist looks upon mind as a function of matter, the idealist upon matter as but an idea in mind.

There is a type of man who is intensely concentrated on this world around him, ever seeking to explore that world more fully, to discover and observe more facts about it, so that ultimately, by learning the laws governing that outer universe, mankind may gain a control over its environment. That type of man may be of the noblest, may be utterly dedicated to the service of humanity, willing to sacrifice life itself in the pursuit of truth, ready to be tortured and burnt at the stake in adherence to that which he knows to be true, and yet, in his intense and absorbed interest in the physical universe, he will very likely come to a solution of duality by recognizing only matter as real and looking upon spirit or life as a by-product, an epiphenomenon.

There is a materialism, in the ethical sense of the word, which is synonymous with a coarse indulgence in the material pleasures of life ; the man who desires but wealth and pleasure, food, drink and material comfort is in that sense a materialist. We should distinguish such a materialism sharply from a true philosophical materialism ; the philosophical materialist may be ascetic in his mode of life, dedicated to others, utterly forgetful of himself in his endeavours to improve the lot of human kind, yet, in his approach to the fundamental problem of duality, he will consider the world of spirit, life or consciousness as vague and unreal, and proclaim matter to be the only and final reality, mind or consciousness being but a result of material processes. In his observation of the world around he sees that, when the material form is destroyed or impaired, life or consciousness no longer manifests itself and his conclusion is that with the destruction of the form the life which was its result has ceased to be also. To him human character is but the outcome of the functioning of the body ; can he not prove that, when certain glands are atrophied or do not function properly, the character of the person in question changes accordingly, whereas the implanting of a fresh gland will restore the previous characteristics ?

In this materialistic view of the universe the ultimate reality is the atom, the unit of matter. Yet when we ponder over the latest contributions of physics towards the nature of matter, when we read of the ultimate atom as a form of energy, charges of negative electricity moving round a positive core, we may well ask if the materialistic solution of the problem of duality can any longer be called materialistic. The materialist's definition of the ultimate material unit and the idealist's definition of the ultimate spiritual unit are not as different as we would expect. And who shall say that what one calls the monad and what the other calls the atom are not one and the same thing ?

Thus, in a materialistic monism, the world of matter around us is seen as the one and only reality, life or consciousness as but a by-product of physical processes.

Very different is the solution of that type of man who is intensely concentrated on the world within. With some the cause of this may be a certain world-shyness, a fear for a material world and for their fellowmen which causes them to shrink back into themselves ; the idealism of such, however, is but a pseudo-idealism. Yet we must not underrate the measure in which failure to cope with the powerful material world surrounding man influences his outlook upon that world. World-negation and world-denial have but too often been the retreat from a world which was too much for man.

There is on the other hand a true idealism, which is rooted in an intense realization of life, consciousness or mind and its creative activity. That which absorbs the idealist most is not the diversity of material forms, not their accurate observation and classification, but the power of life or consciousness over these forms, the fact that in all evolution we can recognize a dynamic, creative principle moulding form from within, above all the outstanding fact that man himself can re-create this world of matter around him, can rise triumphantly over his environment. Thus the importance and reality of that outer world retreat into the background ; life, spirit, or mind becomes the ultimate reality, matter or form but an idea existing in a mind. The objects surrounding us in the world which appears to us so real are denied an objective reality and are but seen as images or ideas arising either in our own mind or the mind of some superior Being. Minds and their ideas are the supreme reality in an idealistic monism, the idealist denies reality to the material world, looks upon it as secondary and upon mind or spirit as primary.

There are many shades, both of materialism and idealism, but the characteristics given above are typical for most ; they solve the problem of duality by denying the reality of one of its two terms and presenting that as but an aspect or by-product of the other.

MATTER AND SPIRIT AS ' ASPECTS '

There is, however, a third way in which unity has been sought and that is by looking upon the two, matter and spirit, or life and form, as opposite aspects of one neutral Reality, neither spirit nor matter. As the two poles of a magnet, the one positive and the other negative, so are the two eternally opposed aspects of the one supreme Reality. This view appeals to us instinctively, because in our daily experience so many things show this same duality of opposites manifesting as male and female, positive and negative, action and reaction, attraction and repulsion. Whether our response to such an appeal is philosophically justified we shall see presently; for the moment our aim is but to present this third approach to the mystery of duality which considers spirit and matter as opposite aspects of supreme reality. It is this doctrine which in Hindu philosophy we find represented by the Sankhya philosophy and which permeates the teachings of the Bhagavad Gita. Thus in its thirteenth discourse we read of ' the beginningless, supreme Eternal, called neither being nor non-being,' and a little further it is said :

> Know thou that matter (Prakriti) and Spirit (Purusha) are both without beginning and know thou also that modifications and qualities are all matter-born.
>
> Matter is called the cause of the generation of causes and effects ; Spirit is called the cause of the enjoyment of pleasure and pain.

Here it is possible for spirit to influence matter or matter to affect spirit because they are aspects of one Reality ; they have an Essence in common and through that which they have in common the one can influence the other.

It is this latter view which we find also in theosophical literature, such as Bhagavan Das's book *The Science of Peace* and Dr. Besant's *Introduction to the Science of Peace ;* here ' Self ' and ' Not-Self ' are the terms given to the ultimate realities—there is an abstract universal Self and an abstract universal Not-Self, the *Pratyagatma* and the *Mulaprakriti.*

Thus in Dr. Besant's work, *A Study in Consciousness*, we read :

> All is separable into ' I ' and ' Not I,' the ' Self ' and the
> ' Not-Self.' Every separate thing is summed up under one
> or other of the headings, SELF or NOT-SELF. There is nothing
> which cannot be placed under one of them. SELF is Life,
> Consciousness ; NOT-SELF is Matter, Form. (p. 6.)

And again :

> We think of a separate something we call consciousness, and
> ask how it works on another separate something we call matter.
> There are no such two separate somethings, but only two
> drawn-apart but inseparate aspects of THAT which, without
> both, is unmanifest, which cannot manifest in the one or the
> other alone, and is equally in both. There are no fronts without
> backs, no aboves without belows, no outsides without insides,
> no spirit without matter. They affect each other because
> inseparable parts of a unity, manifesting as a duality in space
> and time. (pp. 35-36.)

In this view everything belongs either to the universal Self
or the universal Not-Self ; the universal Self and universal
Not-Self form two real divisions to one or other of which
all created things belong.

This solution of the problem of duality again appears in
many different forms and interpretations, of these the one
expressed in the *Bhagavad Gita* and *The Science of Peace* is
philosophically and ethically the most valuable. Where the
deeper interpretation such as we find in those works is lacking,
the third view degenerates into a superficial theory of two
eternal aspects, spirit and matter which in man are eternally
manifest as the animal, the body, on one side, and spirit, the
mind on the other. It is clear that in such a misunderstood
duality of aspects man's mode of life must be one which
strikes a happy medium between spirit and matter, a compromise between the God within and the beast without.
In this superficial interpretation the duality of aspects is

looked upon as unchanging, whereas in the theosophical interpretation quoted above the two aspects are seen in the supreme reality of the creative Rhythm in which there is a return of spirit or self to itself, a conquest of body by mind, a very much superior ethical result from that which we find in the superficial interpretation.

However that may be, in some form or other, whether as parallelism, pre-established harmony or duality of aspects, the third approach to the problem of duality appears in a multitude of doctrines and philosophical theories. There are indeed many forms of each of the three main theories, each form presenting special features or qualifications profoundly affecting the standpoints presented above. Even so the three theories described are the main paths of philosophical approach to the problem of duality.

THE PROBLEM ITSELF ERRONEOUS

Most of the theories offering a solution for the problem of duality in our universe, unhesitatingly accept the problem as it stands and apply their intellectual powers to solve the difficulty which is presented to it ; they but too often neglect first to analyze the problem itself, the question as propounded, and to see whether the problem is correctly formulated. Let us then first analyze the duality which seems so evident to us and see how we come to conclude that there is indeed an objective universe, a world of matter without, and a world of spirit or life within.

We have seen in a previous chapter that the universe appearing around us is the image produced in our consciousness by ultimate Reality. When we dissociate this world-image from the consciousness which produced it, when we externalize it and make of it an objective, outside world, entirely apart from our consciousness, we create a gulf which separates our objectivated world-image from the consciousness that produced it and in that separation we produce the problem of the relation of two apparently separate things— the material universe around us and our consciousness within. That apparent duality then becomes the basis of our dual universe and on that basis are erected the different questions and answers concerning it.

But in philosophy we have no right to accept as sacrosanct any problem which our intellect or our daily experience imposes upon us ; on the contrary, it is our duty first to analyze and study the problem and see whether or not error and illusion have crept into the problem itself. We do but compromise ourselves when we attempt to answer a problem which has in it the element of error, we must first purify it of that error and then we may find it possible to approach reality.

In our interpretation of reality, our world-image, we undoubtedly experience a self within and a world of not-self without. This experience is real enough for us, but to assign to the Absolute a Self, which posits a Not-Self opposite to itself, is to transfer the illusions of our world-image consciousness into our philosophical investigation. In the Absolute, in ultimate Reality there is no such thing as a universal abstract Self, neither is there a universal Not-Self ; self and not-self are concepts which have no place in the world of Reality, they are experiences of the individual creature in the world of the relative ; to transfer them from that world of relativity into the world of the Absolute is a philosophical heresy. Neither can we look upon the two, universal Self and universal Not-Self, as two main divisions, to one or other of which all things belong ; we shall see presently that there is nothing which is either self or not-self *in itself ;* things but *appear* as self or not-self to us; self and not-self are experiences relative to ourselves and of value only with relation to the consciousness which experiences them. We may assign a Self Not-Self construction to the Consciousness which informs a universe, the consciousness of a solar Deity or Logos; there we are still in the world of the relative. To transfer them, however, or rather attempt to transfer them, into the world of Reality, into the world of the Absolute, is impossible. They have no place there, they are flowers of illusion which cannot live in the world of Reality; when we speak of a universal Self we do not speak of an ultimate reality but of an abstract idea which we ourselves distil from our daily experience.

Thus the first ghost to be laid is that of the antithesis of Self and Not-Self, of an objective universe without and a world of consciousness within. These are but concepts born of illusion and in our approach to reality we must overcome them first.

It is of interest to see how in modern physics the problem of duality has been overcome. The problem here concerns the conception of mass or matter on the one side and of force or energy on the other. Here, too, there have been attempts at reconciliation which tried to solve the duality by reducing one of the two terms to but a form of the other. Thus, on the one hand, we find the idea of force reduced to that of mass, Hertz saying definitely that what we denote by the names of force and energy is nothing more than the action of mass or motion; on the other hand we find the atoms explained, as for instance by Boscovich, as being but ' centres of energy,' thus reducing all mass or matter to a form of energy or force. Lately, however, the old and time-honoured antithesis of matter and energy has been questioned and the two are shown to be convertible, one into the other. Inertia, hitherto the outstanding characteristic of mass, is seen to be possessed

also by energy, the inertia for very high velocities being found
to vary with the velocity. Modern physics thus recognizes
a mass of pure electro-magnetic origin, varying with the
velocity. Again, the breaking up of the atom releases energy
and one of the possibilities of modern physics is the liberation
of that energy appearing to us as matter, in which liberation
that same matter ceases to exist as before. We may safely
say that the new physics is thus transcending the old problem
of the duality between matter and energy, not by reducing
one to a function of the other, but by showing that they are
mutually convertible.

Superficially it may seem strange that science, which deals
with the world of phenomena should be able to overcome the
problem of duality or at least come to recognize that the
duality, so sharply defined in classical physics, is a fiction.
But then we must not forget that modern physics is able to
transcend its previous limitations by virtue of the new mathematics which it uses in its calculations and that in these new
mathematics as well as in the theory of relativity based on
them, the illusion which would make absolute that which is
relative, has been overcome.

We must then cease to be fascinated by the problem of
duality either in its scientific or its philosophical presentation,
but, laying aside the questions, born of illusion, approach
that Reality, where the questions are superseded in the
experience of things as they are.

THE EXPERIENCE IN THE WORLD OF THE REAL

Let us then once again withdraw from the contemplation
of our own world-image and turn inwards through our centre
of consciousness, entering the world of the Real. This should
be done not only in thought, but in reality ; only thus can
we experience in ourselves that which, when expressed in

words, seems but an intellectual paradox. Whenever we try to approach the reality of some problem in the world of the Real we should by gradual and slow stages withdraw our consciousness from the contemplation of our world-image, turn it inwards and, through the void where there is no content of consciousness, pass into the world of Reality.

Here we are no longer conscious of anything ; we are all things. When, in the world of Reality, we experience things as they are, there is no trace anywhere of either spirit or matter ; there is not a certain group of things which is labelled ' matter ' or ' not-self ' and another group which is labelled ' self ' in that world of Reality. There the entire distinction appears meaningless ; it is but our relative being which, in our daily experience, makes us look upon certain things as being in themselves matter and upon others as in themselves spirit or Self. In the world of the Real we find no such differences, all things there are essentially the same, an atom of matter as well as a living being. They are all modes of the Absolute and their differences are not differences in being, but only in fullness of realization. Nowhere in this world of reality do we find a trace of a universal Self or a universal Not-Self ; these are but intellectual concepts distilled from our daily experience. The piece of stone which appears to me as not-self in my world image and the consciousness which appears to me as self in that same world-image are here experienced as essentially the same, there is nothing to mark one as self or another as not-self ; the distinction seems a futile one. What we do experience is what has been described already : the simultaneous or eternal presence of all relativity in the Absolute, the ever-lasting, unchanging Reality of all change, growth or becoming, of all creation, which is seen as the very nature of the Absolute. In the world of the Real there is no more reason to call the

Logos of a solar system ' Self ' as there is to call an atom of matter 'not-self ; ' one and all are the eternal relativity of the Absolute which, in them, is limited as the relative.

If then all things are essentially the same why should we experience some as ' matter,' whence comes our awareness of matter as solid and hard, heavy and impenetrable, surrounding us as an outside world ? If all things, whether we call them ' matter ' or ' spirit,' are one and all modes of the Absolute, specifically the same, why then do some of them appear to us as spirit, others as matter, some as self, others as not-self, some as life, others as form ? However much they may be the same in type in the world of the Real there is no doubt, as we explained in the beginning of the chapter, that they appear to us in our daily consciousness as a very real duality, specifically different.

When we consider this question in the light of our experience in the world of Reality we can say the following. It is the action of things in themselves upon us in the world of the Real which is objectivated in our consciousness as our world-image. When the reality which contacts us is superior to us, a fuller realization than we ourselves are, then the result produced in our consciousness is a sense of *increased being ;* we have touched something greater than ourselves and have experienced an increase which we term ' life ' or ' spirit.' When, however, the reality which we contact is of a lesser order than we ourselves are, so that we are unable to express ourselves through it without restriction, then the result in us is *limitation* instead of expansion. This limitation is objectivated in our world-image as that which is outside us, which hems us in, the prison walls by which we are surrounded ;—matter or form. Thus we can characterize matter or form as *the way in which* a lesser reality *appears* to a higher, spirit or life *the way in which* a reality of higher order *appears* to one of lesser order. Spirit and matter are terms denoting a relation between different modes of the Absolute ; as such they are exceedingly useful terms and have a very real meaning. When, however, we look upon them as objective, independently existing realities they become absurd and meaningless.

The very thing which is life to the lesser reality will be form to the higher ; we who are life or self to the cells of our body are form or not-self to some greater being to whom we are but as cells in his body. It is therefore not right to say that a thing is matter or spirit, not-self or self as such, in itself ; it can only be life or form, self or not-self *with regard to something else*, and it is only life or form with regard to that particular thing or group of things. We are once again confronted with the old and fatal mistake of forgetting the relativity of the terms we use and making them into absolute entities. Life and form, spirit and matter, self and not-self are exceedingly valuable terms as long as we understand that they denote but a relationship ; they become dangerous and full of error when we forget this and isolate them on pedestals as independent and essentially different realities. Having done that we can ask as many questions and create as many problems about them as we like ; they one and all remain incapable of solution.

MATTER AND SPIRIT AS RELATIONS

It may help us to a better understanding if we compare the relativity of the terms matter and spirit to a mathematical relation. Since what we call spirit or life is but the relation of a superior mode to an inferior one and matter or form is but the relation of an inferior mode to a superior one we can express the relation in the following way :

DIAGRAM FIVE.
The relativity of spirit and matter.

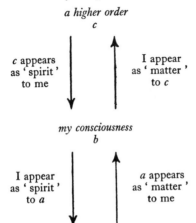

a higher order
c

c appears
as 'spirit'
to me

I appear
as 'matter'
to c

my consciousness
b

I appear
as 'spirit'
to a

a appears
as 'matter'
to me

a lesser order
a

$b = xa$ (my consciousness is as 'spirit' to a)

$b = \dfrac{c}{x}$ (my consciousness is as 'matter' to c)

the relation '$x \times$' denotes 'spirit'

the relation '$\dfrac{}{x}$' denotes 'matter'

'$x \times$' and '$\dfrac{}{x}$' are as meaningless in

themselves as 'spirit' and 'matter.'

If three quantities a, b and c are related in such a way that b is x times a whereas c is x times b then it is clear that b stands in the relation of 'x times' to the quantity a and at the same time will stand in the relation of 'divided by x' to c. Let the relation of 'x times' stand for life or spirit and the relation of 'divided by x' stand for matter, then b will be related as spirit or life to a and at the same time will be related as matter or form to c. If b stands for our human consciousness all things belonging to the a class will stand in the ' divided by x ' relation to it, that is to say they will appear to us as matter, form, whereas all things belonging to the c group will stand in the ' x times ' relation, the spirit or life-relation, to it. We, however, forget all about the relativity of our standpoint and gradually begin to believe that the spirit or ' x times something ' relationship is inherent in c, in the same way as the ' divided by x ' relationship is inherent in a, thus exalting that which is only a relation to an entity with objective existence. Having thus externalized and objectivated to an absolute existence outside of us that which is only a relation to us, we begin to ponder why some things are ' divided by x ' (or matter) in themselves and other things are ' x times ' (or spirit) in themselves, and our problem inevitably is devoid of sense.

Yet this is exactly what we do in daily life when we wonder what causes some things to be matter and others to be spirit, while in reality the true question would be why some things stand in the matter-relation *to us* and other things in the spirit-relation. Nothing is matter or spirit in itself, a thing can only be matter or spirit with regard to something, just as a mathematical quantity cannot be ' x times ' in itself but must always be ' x times something ' and similarly cannot be ' divided by x ' in itself but must always be ' something divided by x.' To objectivate these relations into independent entities, to make them an inherent quality in the quantities a or c is as great an error as to believe that anything is in itself either spirit or matter, life or form. A thing cannot itself be a relation, it can only have a relation to something else. It is our passion for making an absolute entity of that which is only a relationship which causes the difficulty of our spirit-matter problems and the question of duality in general.

We can now see the absurdity of all attempts to proclaim the priority of either of the two relations as being the only real one, as if only the relation of ' x times ' were real and the relation of ' divided by x ' were but a by-product of the other relation. That is what we do when we say that only mind is real and matter is only a result of mind. In the same way it would be unreasonable and even absurd to say that ' x times ' is but a product of ' divided by x,' that only ' divided by x,' or matter, was real and mind a by-product of matter. It is even more unreal to envelop the origin of spirit and matter with a metaphysical religious glamour and say that the Absolute in some mysterious way divides itself into two eternally opposite aspects of spirit and matter, or self and not-self. As well might we make abstract entities out of the relations of ' x times ' and ' divided by x ' and say that the Eternal shows itself in two opposite aspects, one called the ' x times ' aspect and the other one the ' divided by x ' aspect. We show in our very attempts at such explanations the power of the illusion of our world-image over us and our subjection to that original sin of philosophy, which is to make absolute entities out of things which are only relationships. Thus I can but repeat that in attempting to solve the age-long problem of spirit and matter we compromise ourselves philosophically and condemn ourselves not only as being subject to the illusion of our world-image, but as guilty of the crime of *lèse majesté*, which we commit when we try to transfer our illusions into the world of ultimate Reality.

Once again, our experience of certain things as matter, as form, as a solid objective universe around us and of other things as life or spirit within is a very real one indeed, and not for a moment should we make the mistake of trying to deny the reality of our *experience* of duality. But let us never forget that this apparent duality is but due to *the way in which things appear to us*, due to the relation in which certain things stand *to us* and affect *us* as increased being, spirit, or as limitation of being, matter, and that the same thing which is form to us may well be life with regard to something else and that we ourselves who are spirit with regard to our body, may well be matter with regard to some superior entity. Matter and spirit are terms denoting a relation, not abstract realities in themselves.

It is now clear how body may act on mind or mind on body, how force or energy may affect mass and mass resist energy. In the world of reality there is neither spirit nor matter, life nor form ; there are only modes of being of and in the Absolute. That some of those, when contacted by a human consciousness, should appear as either of the relationships mentioned is but due to the place of our human consciousness in the scale of all relative things ; when our place in that scale changes and we grow from human to superhuman beings these relations change with us. Yet in their eternal reality things have not changed at all, it is but in *our experience of them*, in our relation to them that they gain their meaning as matter, spirit, life or form. Our interpretations of Reality may vary, Reality remains and is ever unaffected by the names we give to the experience which we have of it.

CHAPTER SEVEN

THE PHANTOM OF EVIL

*After this I saw God in a Point, that is to say, in mine under-
standing,—by which sight I saw that He is in all things. I
beheld and considered, seeing and knowing in sight, and with a
soft dread, and thought : What is sin?*—JULIAN OF NORWICH.

THE OPPOSITES, GOOD AND EVIL

OF all the terrors which man has created for himself there
is none more potent than that of Evil. From the earliest
times, when primitive man lived in a world peopled by awful
mysteries, malignant entities ever seeking to oppose and
harm him, to the present day, Evil in some form or other has
appeared as an objective reality, a power opposing good, evil
in its very nature, sometimes even as a being, a Lord of Evil.
The ancient Egyptian thought of evil as threatening him in
many strange forms ; we need but read the Book of the Dead
to see how profoundly the Egyptian's life, especially after
death, was dominated by fears of strange and evil beings,
hard to overcome, and harmless only to him who could repel
them by the magic of ceremonial incantation. There was,
in the religious outlook of ancient Egypt, no doubt about the
reality of evil ; was there not eternal strife between Osiris,
Isis and Horus, and the evil One, Set or Typhon ?

In the religion of ancient Persia this dualism of good and
evil is even more pronounced ; life is seen as an eternal battle
between the power of Good, Ahura Mazda, and the power

of Evil, Anra Mainyu. The follower of Zarathustra looked upon himself as the champion of Ahura Mazda, a soldier fighting under Him in His great struggle to overcome the evil One. There is no doubt in Zoroastrianism about the objective reality of evil, good and evil are an eternal duality, two distinct powers, battling for supremacy.

Zoroastrian dualism had a profound influence on Jewish religious ideas; in the Old Testament too evil appears personified; Satan, the Prince of Evil, is the Enemy of the human race. In Christianity this conception of a personified Evil has remained the dismal heritage of Jewish tradition; however little justification there is to be found in Christ's actual teachings for the conception of an objectively real evil; the early Christians, in their fear of a world full of temptation were only too ready to recognize the sly cunning of the Enemy of the race in the beauty of the world surrounding them, where a little introspection might have shown them their own weakness in being unable to rejoice in that beauty without becoming enslaved by it.

In the history of philosophy we find of necessity a continual endeavour to deal with this problem of evil which, more than any other philosophical problem, affects us directly in our daily life. Here certainly we are not dealing with a vague abstraction, of interest only to the subtle theologian or the philosopher, far removed from daily life. The experience of evil as a power opposing good, the realization in ourselves of an incessant struggle between lofty aspiration and earthly desire is too real to be denied. All day long we are conscious in some form or other, on the one hand, of our own volition and determination, on the other hand, of a power resisting us and even enticing us away from the goal we set ourselves. The literature of all nations and of all times is replete with the theme of this struggle between good and evil, noble aspiration and ignoble desire in man's life. Few indeed are the works of literature in which that theme, in one form or another, is absent ; the life of every human being is but a chapter in that eternal epic of the struggle between good and evil. The consciousness of this struggle has hardly ever been expressed more dramatically than in St. Paul's *Epistle to the Romans*, where the Apostle says :

> For the good that I would I do not : but the evil which I would not, that I do.
> Now if I do that I would not, it is no more I that do it, but sin that dwelleth in me.
> I find then a law, that, when I would do good, evil is present with me.
> For I delight in the law of God after the inward man : but I see another law in my members, warring against the law of my mind, and bringing me into captivity to the law of sin which is in my members.
> O wretched man that I am ! who shall deliver me from the body of this death ? (*Romans*, vii. 19-25.)

It is but natural that, like St. Paul, we should instinctively localize evil in our physical nature, the ' body of sin ' of which he speaks ; we somehow feel that the tendency for evil is inherent in matter as such, and in many a philosophy, even in Platonism and in Neo-Platonism, it is matter and its evils which obscure the good of the spirit. Yet, if we come to analyze our wrong actions we cannot attribute them simply to our body and its tendencies, we ourselves must give our sanction before an action is done and hence we are conscious of a sense of guilt or even shame when we have done that which is not right. If our wrong-doing were merely inherent in the body we should not have that sensation in ourselves of having done wrong ; we know but too well that, at the moment of our action, we willed to do that very thing even though we knew all the time that it was wrong. Granted then that evil in us lies in a wrong use of the will even then the question remains what it is in man that makes him consent to do the wrong thing. It is but a philosophical platitude to say that all things are good and that evil is but the absence of good ; this intellectual ingenuity may sound reasonable, but it means nothing. We know only too well that evil or wrong-doing is not a mere absence of good, not a colourless neutrality, but rather something positively different from goodness, apparently its very opposite.

What then is the origin of this evil, whether inherent in matter as such, in the human will as a tendency, or personified in the Prince of Evil, who wages a perpetual warfare against the Power of God ? In Christian Theology especially do we find it difficult to account for the existence of evil whilst looking upon God as the Creator of all things. How can a Creator be omnipotent and good and yet create evil or allow it to originate ? Either God created evil with the intention to do so, in which case we cannot call Him good, or else He could not help creating it or, even worse, evil has an objective existence apart from the divine Being, eternally opposed to Him, in both of which cases we can hardly call God omnipotent. It does not help us to say, as is often done, that he gave free will to man, power to choose either good or evil, and that man chose wrongly. If man could choose wrongly that inclination for evil must have been created in him, had he been created all good, he could only have chosen good, and thus the problem remains the same. Even less can we look upon man's deliberate choice of evil as an unforeseen misfortune in the scheme of things, something of which the Creator had not thought ; in that case where is divine Omniscience ?

We can see the inability of orthodox Christian theology to deal with the problem in the following words from the much used *Manual of Theology* by Dr. Strong :

Evil is a fact as things are now, but we believe that it was not a *necessary* part of the scheme. We see how God over-rules it for good, how He uses it in the education of mankind ; we know that, through His Son, He saves us from it ; and the possibility of it seems to our minds to belong to the exercise of free choice. Further than this we doubt whether the human mind can go. But the mystery which remains insoluble is after all a metaphysical or intellectual mystery ; there is no room for doubt either as to God's Hatred of evil, or His Power to overcome it : the Incarnation is the measure both of His Hatred of evil and of His Power. (p. 226.)

Here, as elsewhere, we find the reality of evil accepted unhesitatingly ; instead of first analyzing the problem and seeing whether it is justified or whether in the problem itself there are misconceptions, man wearies and tortures his brain in attempting to solve that which cannot be solved. Our explanations or solutions may be ever so logical, we do but compromise ourselves in our attempts to solve a problem which is essentially wrong. Above all, however, we must guard against empty phrases such as ' evil is but the absence of good,' or ' there is no evil but ignorance,' or, worst of all, ' in this world of opposites we cannot have good without evil as little as we can have light without darkness.' All such phrases are empty of meaning ; when we do evil we know but too well that there is more in it than ignorance, ignorance alone would not give us a feeling of guilt, shame or even self-contempt. Our experience of evil, our consciousness of doing wrong is real enough, to deny that would be absurd, but to accept therefore the problem of evil as a real problem, to be solved as it stands, is worse. Let us then lay aside the problem for a while and enter the world of Reality, where we can know things as they are.

GOOD, EVIL AND REALITY

When we enter the world of the Real we do not leave one world for another, we do not withdraw for a moment from physical world which is less real into a spiritual world of a higher reality. That is a misconception against which we must guard incessantly ; there is but one World and that is the world of the Real, in that world are all things, also those which we call ' physical objects.' Thus we do not forsake one world for another, we do not enter a higher or loftier realm, we enter the world of things-as-they-are and in that world we experience the reality of that which in our world-image appears as our physical universe.

When, in the light of this experience in the world of Reality we consider the problem of the origin and existence of evil, we see that the problem has become empty of meaning, there is nothing in the world of Reality which we can call evil. Neither can we there call anything good, the words ' good ' and ' evil ' have no meaning whatever in the experience of Reality ; we experience things as they are and cannot say of them that they are either good or evil in themselves, they are what they are and their being is their justification. We can now understand why Julian of Norwich, in the account of the supreme mystical experience of her life, says that she beheld God in all things and, in beholding Him thus, thought ' with a soft dread ' what is sin ? To one who had been brought up in the dogmatism of mediaeval Christianity with its emphasis on man's sinfulness and the reality of evil as a power in his life, it must indeed have come like a shock to find that, in the world of divine Illumination, the very word ' sin ' or ' evil ' had become void of meaning. In the supreme Experience we are no longer in the world of relativity hence good and evil have become words without meaning.

As little as we could say that anything is in itself either spirit or matter can we say that anything in the world of Reality is either good or evil. We found matter and spirit to be *ways* in which things as they are appear *to us* as human beings and we have seen that it depends on our place in the scale of all things whether a thing appears to us as spirit or as matter. It was our forgetfulness of our personal relation in those conceptions of spirit and matter which caused us to look upon them as absolute realities, independent of our human consciousness, instead of as relations to that consciousness.

Our psychological procedure with regard to good and evil is much the same ; in our contact with things-as-they-are in the world of the Real some appear to us, or are experienced by us, as good and others as evil ; these two, good and evil, thus denote the *way* in which realities appear *to us* at our human level. So far no illusion, no danger of error, has crept into our conceptions ; our experience of certain things as good and of others as evil is real enough. But when we forget that these terms, good and evil, do but denote the way in which things-in-themselves appear to us, when we make objective realities out of things which are but relations to us, then we have created monstrosities which henceforth will ever haunt our philosophical atmosphere. Good and evil are real enough as relations of things to us, human beings, to absolutize them is to create insuperable and insoluble problems.

We shall presently see the meaning of the terms good and evil in the world of relativity, where they not only have a profound significance, but in which they are a very real experience for every one of us. At present, however, we are considering the problem in the light of ultimate Reality and there neither good nor evil have meaning ; they are not ultimate realities. We find many who are willing to accept that evil is not an ultimate reality ; we have already discussed the philosophical platitude of saying that evil is but the absence of good. But there are few who in the quest of ultimate Reality are able to relinquish entirely their anxious clinging to the world of relativity ; they will recognize that evil has no objective existence, but surely, they say, good has a real and objective existence, do we not speak of God Himself as good, the supreme Good indeed ? Would not our whole life, the entire moral structure of our social order collapse when we no longer recognize the ultimate reality of the Good ?

If we fear to take leave of the familiar features of our world-image we had better not embark on the quest of reality. Ultimate Reality is not conditioned by any results which we may right or wrongly fear for ourselves or the social order in which we live, ultimate Reality *is*. And in this Reality nothing is good as little as anything is evil ; if we wish to call this absolute and ultimate reality ' God ' then we certainly cannot say that this God is good. We can only apply the word ' good ' to beings or things in the world of the relative ; thus we can speak of the Deity of a solar system as being good, He to us is indeed the supreme Good, of Him we can say that He is Love, Goodness, and whatever other qualifications we may use in attempting to describe the supreme Being for this our universe in the world of relativity. But none of these terms can ever apply to absolute Reality, the Absolute is truly ' beyond good and evil.' To think of ultimate Reality as ' good ' is as unphilosophical as to think of it as ' spiritual,' it is neither the one nor the other, it is That which to us appears as matter or spirit, good or evil.

Let us, however, guard against the equally serious, if not more serious, mistake, of trying to transfer the Absolute into the world of the relative and to look upon ' being beyond good and evil ' as a possible achievement or ideal in human evolution. Ultimate Reality is beyond good and evil, only in our experience of ultimate Reality are we beyond good and evil, the moment we enter the world of the Relative good and evil are very real indeed.

GOOD AND EVIL IN THE WORLD OF THE RELATIVE

If then in the world of the Absolute nothing is either good or evil, while in the world of the relative we are painfully aware that some things are as evil as others are good, what is it that causes us to experience some things as evil and others as good ?

Let us begin by realizing that at every point of the vast scheme of evolution certain things are right and fitting for the evolving creature, others are not. Thus certain conditions of life were right for the prehistoric reptile ; when, however, the winged creature evolved it needed and utilized conditions of life very different from those which were right for the reptile. The same holds good for different creatures at the present time ; water is as right and fitting an environment for the fish as air is for the bird and earth is for the mole. For each of these the environment of the other would be fatal ; that which is right for the one is wrong for the other ; to say that any environment is right or wrong in itself would be to forget the relativity involved and make an absolutistic absurdity out of that which is a relative truth.

This conception of relative fitness and ' rightness ' is found again in the life of every individual creature in the species ; that which is right and necessary for the egg is no longer right for the young bird, and the environment of the helpless fledgling is no longer suitable for the full-grown animal. It is the same in our human life ; conditions which are right for the infant would be absurd for the youth and those which suit a grown-up man might well kill a growing child. Relativity reigns everywhere ; what is right for one is wrong for the other, nothing is right or wrong in itself.

Proceeding from the physiological to the psychological we find the same to be true. The scheme of life which suits a certain type and is the very condition of its self-expression would be a hindrance and an impossibility both for a less evolved and for a further evolved type. There is a scheme of life which we can express in rules of right and wrong for each stage of evolution and that which is right for one stage is generally wrong for another.

In Hindu philosophy this fact is taught as the doctrine of *dharma*, a word which is variously translated as ' duty,' ' law,' ' right,' or ' virtue,' words which seem far enough apart, but which yet are contained in the full meaning of the word ' dharma.' There is no English word to translate all that dharma means, the nearest translation would perhaps be ' the Right,' that which is lawful, right and fitting. This rightness or fitness would then be *law* in social procedure, *duty* in the life of the individual, *truth* in philosophical and religious matters, but always the central idea would be that which is right and fitting. Thus, in the *Manu-Smrti* we find it said that there is a different dharma for each of the yugas, or periods of evolution, that is to say that at every stage of evolution a different set of laws, customs, and even ethical precepts, are right and fitting for a group of human beings.

In Hindu philosophy we find the conception of dharma not only used for the nation or race but also for the individual. As a consequence of the doctrine of reincarnation Hinduism knows the caste system in which four castes are recognized, the priests or teachers, the warriors and rulers, the merchant men and artizans and those performing menial labours. Each of the castes represents a stage of evolution and has its own set of rights and duties, its own dharma; what is right for one caste is wrong for the other, but no scheme of life can be looked upon as right or wrong in itself. Within each caste again the doctrine of dharma is pursued and the life of a member of the higher castes is divided into four stages or ashramas, those of the disciple, the householder, the dweller in the woods, and the homeless wanderer. Each of these stages has its own set of rights and duties corresponding to the mentality of the period in life of which they are the expression. Thus that which is the right or duty of the disciple, is wrong for the householder or for the dweller in the woods, and no scheme of life or set of rules is wrong or right in itself.

There is then a dharma, or right and fitting scheme of things, for our humanity at the present day, expressing the spirit of the Age, differing of course for every race and every nation. Even within each nation there are necessarily some who are in advance of others and some who are behind the general level of evolution ; the first will be beyond the dharma of their nation, the others have not yet quite reached the level of which it is the expression. Yet there is a vast majority in a nation or race whose level of evolution is about the same and for whom about the same rules of life hold good. This general dharma of our Age is expressed in our moral and ethical conceptions which embody that which in these days we hold to be good or evil, right or wrong. It is inevitable that some of our social conventions and moral customs lag behind the evolving spirit of man of which they were the expression, consequently they are often but a burden to those who are ahead of their times. Even so there is a morality, a conception of certain things as good and others as evil which belongs to this age, just as every age in the past has had its morality.

It is not difficult to see that for primitive man, who was but just evolving from a state of unconscious unity, self-assertion was as right and necessary as it becomes wrong and superfluous when man returns to Unity, where the law of his life is renunciation, self-surrender and service. We are at present emerging from a period of excessive individualism and in our social life self-assertion is still the rule and renunciation the exception. Yet in our ethical code we recognize service to our fellow-men as right and noble, selfishness as wrong and ignoble ; the ethics which we admire and strive to realize are thus always a little in advance of the general practice, just as on the other hand many conventions and customs have become rigid forms which the spirit of man has outgrown.

We can readily see that there must be a morality as far beyond our ideals of the present age as ours are beyond those of primitive man. Thus the ethics of the Sermon on the Mount are the rule of life for those who are approaching the stature of the Christ-man, they are as yet in advance of the spirit of the Age and could hardly yet be introduced as a social code. Christ taught them to his disciples, and those who are willing to follow in his footsteps try to practise these teachings. But if it became the duty of all to give their coat also when their shirt was taken the wicked would flourish exceedingly and soon enslave the good, the least moral among nations would trample on the noblest, ignorance and greed would enthrone themselves in the seats of the rulers of men. The morality of the man in the street or of the nations of to-day is not yet the morality of the disciple of Christ, that morality would fit them as little as a morality which they have outgrown.

Yet we instinctively feel admiration and respect for the morality for which we may not yet be ready and disdain the morality which we have outgrown ; even though we may not yet try to live according to the ethics of the Sermon on the Mount we recognize their exalted level and would fain look upon them as absolute and ultimate morality, as right in themselves. The reason for this may well be that the morality of the Sermon on the Mount is the morality which will be ours when we near the completion of our evolutionary cycle. In the world of the Real we are even now that which, in evolution, we do but gradually become, and some glimpse of what we are to be some day is caught by us at times and makes us see as the highest morality that which expresses the nobility which one day we shall achieve. We, however, live in forgetfulness of our true nobility and allow ourselves to be enslaved and dominated by the bodies which are but our instruments, our servants. Thus the morality which is too far advanced for us as long as we are thus enslaved may yet awaken in us a response of admiration and respect. Yet even the highest morality which we can recognize must of necessity be relative, the expression of a certain level of evolution ; beyond it again there may be conceptions of right and wrong, good and evil, the very nature of which we could not understand at present, even if they were explained to us. Without exception, therefore, *good and evil are terms denoting the relation of certain things, events or beings, to us at our present level of evolution.*

OUR SOCIAL CODE OF ETHICS

We should make a serious mistake if we thought that the fact that nothing is good or evil in itself and that there is no absolute good or absolute evil, makes ethical endeavour impossible or superfluous in our lives. Most certainly nothing is good or evil in itself ; good and evil have no reality as entities or powers, yet even so they are very real as relations to us and the most important fact remains that in our lives certain things *stand to us* in the relation we call ' good,' others in the relation we call ' evil,' certain things are right for us, being a fitting expression of what we are at the present moment, other things are wrong and do not fit. That which fits we call ' right,' that which does not fit we call ' wrong ; ' in the use of the words ' good ' and ' evil ' we go a little further in that and are wont to call evil the scheme of life which we have outgrown, good both the scheme of life which is ours and that which we have not yet reached. Even so they remain terms denoting a relation of things to us.

What makes our conceptions of good and evil even more difficult to analyze is that many of the things, which we call evil or wicked or which, on the other hand, we suffer as right and acceptable, are but so to us because of the conventions and social customs in which we have been brought up. Thus we call it evil and wicked to torture an animal, yet sanction such torture when it is called sport ; we do not hesitate to kill and maim millions of animals for the sake of amusement or vanity while we feel a righteous indignation when we see a man beat his dog. Yet, those same things which we sanction as legalized cruelty would be looked upon, and are looked upon, with uttermost horror in Buddhist countries where harm done to any creature is considered to be always wrong and is never legalized under the name of sport or sanctioned by the demands of fashion.

On the other hand there are things which to us seem immoral, of which we think with horror and which yet in other civilizations were or are customary and not immoral. Thus we look upon the Greek conception of life as a noble and lofty one, yet in ancient Greece certain social customs were common and accepted which at the present day we condemn as criminal. Again we are accustomed to the marriage of one man to one woman and look with horror upon the custom of polygamy, even though the increase of divorce makes the dividing line between modern marriage and either polygamy or polyandry but a slight one. Even so, in theory we condemn them. Yet these forms of marriage are still looked upon as moral in various races and it might well be that, if we had been born among them and been accustomed to them from childhood, they would not in any way strike us as immoral. In fact, if presently another greater and more terrible world-war should break out, in which modes of destruction were to be used, more horribly efficient even than those we have known in the last war, the number of men killed might well be so overwhelming that polygamy would become a necessity to save the race, and no doubt we should soon get used to that which we now consider with horror as immoral. After all we need not necessarily call King Solomon an immoral man because he happened to have several hundred wives, it was his misfortune rather than his fault, and, in the social outlook of his day, which we admire sufficiently to make it part of our sacred Scriptures, his excessively numerous household was not in any way looked upon as a sign of wickedness or immorality. Custom too is relative, but, because it is custom, we forget its relativity and look upon things as absolutely and in themselves right or wrong when in many cases they are but so to us through custom.

Let no one be deceived into thinking that the knowledge that good and evil are but relative implies a relaxation of ethical effort and an indifference to social progress. The danger of any attempt to state the reality of things, which, of necessity, is above the intellect, is that, since the exposition, can never be a complete or a correct one, those who cannot themselves transcend the intellect will attempt to digest intellectually that which belongs to the world of the Real and in doing so will inevitably misunderstand or even distort that which they cannot grasp. It might seem a logical conclusion to say ' if nothing is good in itself, if all good and evil are but relative, there is no longer a standard of ethics and behaviour, and whatever I do, however wicked or evil it may seem to some one else, may well be right and good for me. Who is there to impose upon me an absolute code of social ethics and individual morality when I know that all morality is relative, that good and evil do but denote relations ? And if there is no ultimate and absolute good what incentive is there left for those who try in uttermost sacrifice to improve social conditions, why reform if even the highest good we can see is but relative ? '

It is in such distortions that we see the utter inability of the intellect and of logical reasoning to appreciate reality. Certainly, good and evil are but terms denoting a relation and are not absolute realities in themselves, but that does not for a moment make ethical demand for the individual less stringent or the need for social reform less urgent. Though we can never speak of any behaviour as being absolutely and in itself good, this does not mean that nothing can be said to be good, moral or ethical at all for a community. On the contrary, if the relativity of good and evil is understood it follows inevitably that there *must* be a code of ethics and of behaviour which for a particular community at a particular time is right and any transgression of which is evil and wrong. In a similar way the relativity of good and evil does in no wise mean that social conditions must ever be stagnant ; social evolution remains a reality and the work of the social reformer will ever be the expression of the principles of the next stage in evolution.

Thus the very thought of relativity gives power and authority to the code of ethics of any community since it shows us why, for that community, such a code of ethics is right, must be right. There must of necessity be exceptions in every community, there are always those who are either beyond the social morality of their time and those who have not yet reached its level. The former will suffer since their own code of ethics will cause them to be the victims of their less evolved fellowmen ; was not Christ Himself done to death by those to whom His principles seemed but blasphemy ? On the other hand, those who are as yet behind the morality of their times will find it hard, if not impossible, to comply with it and, in their transgressions, will lay themselves open to the coercive and corrective measures which all communities institute against those who break their laws.

Even so the criminal laws of a country are never a perfect embodiment of the code of ethics which would be right or fitting for that country ; but too often things are punished severely which hardly seem to deserve such punishment and much is left unpunished which yet calls for correction. It is doubtful whether any community has the right ever to *punish* those who offend against its code of ethics. It is clear that a community has, not only the right, but the duty to protect those who have reached the general level of evolution against the backward ones and to *correct* these backward ones, whom we call criminals, by placing them in an environment where they can be helped to grow to a higher level of morality. Such measures, however severe they may be, are coercive and corrective ; they cannot be called punishment. The idea of a community retaliating on the individual who has done wrong and exacting ' an eye for an eye ' may fit in with the more bloodthirsty ethics of the Old Testament ; it hardly seems suitable for a civilization which protests its belief in One who certainly never taught either punishment or retaliation.

Since the code of right and wrong for a group is not only the expression of the level it has reached in evolution, but already aims at the next stage towards which that group is evolving, morality is ever of a progressive nature, expressing the spirit of the time and also the spirit of the immediate future. Thus the intensity of our endeavour to do the right thing and of our opposition to all that is wrong or evil is strengthened rather than weakened when once we see the truth of the relativity of good and evil, when the phantom of Evil is laid.

CHAPTER EIGHT

THE FREEDOM OF THE WILL

Demand not things to happen as you will, but will them to happen as they do happen and you will live in peace.
EPICTETUS, *Encheiridion.*

FREEDOM AND NECESSITY

IT is doubtful whether, either in philosophy or in theology, there is a subject which has raised more controversy and been productive of more contradictory theories than that of the freedom of the human will. When a moral crisis presents itself in our lives, when we are confronted by the choice between good and evil, are we free to choose either the one or the other? If we are free in our choice what then of causality, of God's foreknowledge of things to come, of predestination and determinism, what of the many indubitable instances of accurate prophecy or premonition? On the other hand, if we are not free to choose what then of moral effort, what of all endeavours to lead a noble life, what of guilt and sin, shame and repentance, reward or punishment? It seems inevitable that the will should either be free or not free, and yet, whichever of the two alternatives we accept, we find ourselves landed in contradictions and difficulties and find our theories incompatible with the facts of our daily experience.

Our nature revolts against the iron slavery of a mechanical necessity, a determinism in which we are but as puppets moved by strings. If we accept such a determinism there seems no reason why we should ever attempt to live nobly ; since everything is determined anyhow and we cannot escape from the grim necessity of an irresistible fate we may as well abandon all struggle and effort, all aspiration and enthusiasm and descend to the level of a purely animal existence.

There is within every one of us a conviction and certainty of freedom, a rebellion against the idea of a necessity that would compel us and from which there is no escape. It is true that it is dangerous to be led by our instinctive convictions, however compelling and deeply rooted they may be ; too often a fundamental instinct is but rooted in illusion. Yet it would be foolish to pass by lightly such a profound conviction as that of freedom ; even if we should be logically convinced of its impossibility it will not be denied and will make itself felt in our life in some way or other.

However adverse we may be to the idea that our entire life, in all its actions and events, is predetermined, there are yet reasons which would seem to make such conclusions inevitable. Nothing ever happens in our experience without a cause, every event can be traced back to the influences that caused it, and should we fail to trace it back in such a way this is due rather to our insufficient knowledge of the causes than to the fact that there were no causes and that the result emerged spontaneously. It cannot be denied that there is a causality of thought, feeling and volition as well as a mechanical causality governing mere physical happenings and we cannot escape the conclusion that, if at any particular moment we could arrest the entire universe, there would be present in it the causes of anything that can ever happen in the future, whether such causes would be of a physical, emotional, mental or spiritual nature. It then seems no longer impossible that everything should be pre-ordained, not perhaps by some inexorable fate, but rather by the causes inherent in nature and in man. In the light of this we can see the theoretical possibility that one, who can contact these causes inherent in things, might consequently be able to know the future and foretell it in detail.

Prophecy has ever been a reality in human history; however abundant false prophecy may have been, one case of accurate prophecy outweighs a thousand cases of pseudo-prophecy. Such a case was that of a famous Scotch seer, whose prophecies are still remembered.

Some centuries ago Coinneach Odhar Fiosaiche, better known as 'the Brahan seer' was born on the Seaforth property in Lewis. He soon became known for his gift of the second sight which, between the years 1630 and 1680 led him to prophesy many future events, some of which undoubtedly did come to pass. The remarkable feature of these prophecies was that not only a single event was prophesied which, by chance, might have come to pass in future days, but that a number of surrounding circumstances were prophesied as well, which convey the impression that the Brahan Seer did not merely see the main event of the prophecy, but had a vision of the general surrounding circumstances at that time as well. Thus one of his prophecies known as 'the Seaforth prediction' or 'The Doom of the House of Kintail,' runs as follows in its quaint wording:

> I see a Chief, the last of his House, both deaf and dumb. He will be the father of four fair sons, all of whom he shall follow to the tomb. He shall live careworn, and die mourning, knowing that the honours of his House are to be extinguished for ever, and that no future Chief of the Mackenzies shall rule in Kintail. After lamenting over the last and most promising of his sons, he himself shall sink into the grave, and the remnant of his possessions shall be inherited by a white-coifed lassie from the East, and she shall kill her sister. As a sign by which it shall be known that these things are coming to pass, there

shall be four great lairds in the days of the last Seaforth (Gair-
loch, Chisholm, Grant, and Raasay), one of whom shall be
buck-toothed, the second hare-lipped, the third half-witted,
and the fourth a stammerer. Seaforth, when he looks round
and sees them, may know that his sons are doomed to death, and
that his broad lands shall pass away to the stranger, and that his
line shall come to an end. (A. Mackenzie, *The Prophecies of
the Brahan Seer*, pp. 74-75.)

The Seaforth prophecy was current in the Highlands for
generations, until, more than a century after it had been
uttered, it came true, even to the quaint details of contempo-
rary events and persons given in it. Nor was that the only
one of the Seer's prophecies which was fulfilled, and always
he not merely predicted some event, but gave surrounding
circumstances in almost minute details.

Reading these and similar prophecies we cannot fail to
come to the conclusion which Prof. Richet gives in *Thirty
Years of Psychical Research*, namely ' that premonition is a
demonstrated fact.' Richet continues as follows (pp. 395-6) :

In certain circumstances not as yet definable, certain
individuals (mostly, though not exclusively, hypnotizable
persons or mediums) can announce events to come, and give
precise details on these events that are not as yet existent ;
details so exact that no perspicuity, no coincidence, and no
chance can account for the prediction.

We are therefore driven to infer that the special, mysterious
faculty that we have called cryptesthesia, whose nature and
modes of action are unknown, is not only manifested for past
and present facts, but also for future ones.

After all, the metapsychic cognition of existing distant facts
is so marvellous that cognition of the future is not so very much
more extraordinary. A knows that B, six hundred miles away,
is drowned. How can A know this ? We have not the least
idea. A announces that B will be drowned to-morrow. It is
only a little more marvellous. In the whole domain of metapsychic lucidity, so profound is the mystery and so impenetrable
the obscurity that a little more or less mystery should not appal
us.

Are we then to conclude that time is only a notion of our defective mental constitution, that the future is irrevocably fated, that free will is an illusion, and that there is no moral responsibility ? Long discussions might be raised on that text. I shall not enter on arguments that pertain more to metaphysics than to metapsychics, nor allow myself to be led into vain speculation. I shall abide in the domain of strict facts. There are indisputable and verified facts of premonition. Their explanation may or may not come later ; meanwhile the facts are there—authenticated and undeniable. *There are premonitions.*

Are these due solely to human intelligence, or to other intelligent forces acting on our minds ? It is impossible to decide. We must be content with exact observation of the facts.

And it would be inexcusably rash to affirm, as I have boldly done, that *there are premonitions*, if abundant and formal proof had not been advanced. This abundant and formal proof has, I think, been given.

If then there are premonitions, if it is certain that there are and have been people who predicted future events of which no foreknowledge, by telepathy or otherwise was possible, and if such predictions, as in the case of the Brahan Seer, were given with a wealth of attendant circumstances, showing almost a vision of some place at a future time, the conclusion indeed seems inevitable that the future is determined even now (how else could it be known at this moment ?) and that our alleged freedom of choice is but an illusion. And yet— we feel free !

ANALYSIS OF THE FREEDOM OF CHOICE

However overwhelming may be the evidence to show that future events are determined even now and can be known by those who have the super-normal faculty we call the gift of prophecy, even so in every one of our actions, in the very fact of our hesitating and deliberating before we decide how to act, we seem to give the lie to necessity and assert our freedom.

When I hold a glass of water in my hand I feel perfectly free either to drink or not to drink, and I should smile at the idea that my choice was not my own decision but a predetermined necessity. Yet we must be very careful not to confuse our *feeling* that we are free to do as we like with the actual freedom of choice. It is a simple experiment in hypnosis to suggest to the subject that the next day at a certain hour he shall desire to drink a glass of water and that on awakening from the hypnotic sleep he shall have forgotten all about this suggestion. When the hour comes the person will feel a natural desire to drink, not different from that which would usually precede the drinking of a glass of water, and if we asked him whether he chose of his own freewill he would answer that he certainly did. Yet in this case we should know for certain that the action was not one of his own free choice, but definitely compelled from without. Thus the feeling of freedom, which is such an important factor in our thoughts on the subject of the freedom of the will, would be present in exactly the same way as when the desire to drink was natural. This proves that it is hard, if not impossible, for us to distinguish between desire and compulsion, and that the argument from the feeling of freedom with which we are so familiar, is not as important as it would seem. It cannot be emphasized sufficiently that in all discussions and thoughts about the question of freedom of the will the fact that we *feel* free to choose in all matters should not carry any weight ; however insistently it makes itself felt, we must be on our guard against sentimental conclusions.

There is a vast amount of confusion to be cleared away before we can approach the problem of freedom at all in a profitable way. Thus our aversion to the idea of predestination is mainly due to the fact that we conceive this to imply a compelling destiny from *without*, which not only shapes our ends, but determines our future in every detail, making us but pawns in its game. This would rule out all effort, struggle, endeavour or aspiration on our part in the life we lead and do away for ever with all ideas of responsibility for good or evil actions done. Yet, when we come to analyze in what way our choice is determined we see that it is not so much a ruthless fate from without which decides us as a self-determination from *within*.

Let us begin with the analysis of a very simple choice, such as whether we shall go out for a walk or not. We feel perfectly free in deciding one way or another, granted that we have no immediate other duties to perform. Yet something must determine my choice, the choice does not make itself and when I analyze what happens before the decision is made I see that a number of outer and inner factors combine to bring it about. The weather may be good or bad, I may be reading a story of absorbing interest and stay at home rather than go out, or again my state of health may decide me toward either the one or the other. Yet all the time I feel perfectly free to choose whatever I will. Apart, however, from the outer factors which go to make up my choice there are factors from within ; my natural inclinations may be towards an outdoor life or towards reading and study, the way in which I have spent the last few days may lead me to seek a different occupation now ; all these are factors working from within, my own disposition of the moment. In my deliberations before the choice is made I unconsciously imagine what it will be like to go out walking, what it will feel like, and on the other hand what it will feel like to be at home ; one or other of the two possibilities will call forth associations of pleasure or displeasure which will finally decide my choice. We might say that at the moment of deciding there is a *constellation* of factors present, both outer circumstances and inner inclinations or associations. There is no question of a merely mechanical process, it is not a determination from without only, outer and inner influences combine to bring about the final result—my choice. Once this choice is made it would be quite possible for one who had a complete knowledge of all the factors at work to reduce the decision made to the influences that brought it about. Notwithstanding my feeling of being entirely free to choose whether I shall go out walking or stay at home to read, my choice is determined by the totality of inner and outer factors present at the moment. And with a sufficient knowledge of those the final decision could be known also.

In more serious decisions a similar process takes place. When I see someone fall into the water there are a number of factors which help to decide whether I shall jump in after him or not. First of all there are factors from without ; in the case of a child I shall certainly attempt to save it. If on the other hand the victim is a man, who may be able to swim, I shall feel inclined to watch events and see whether or not he can save himself. Again, I may either be dressed in a bathing costume and thus feel it to be only a small matter to jump into the water, or on the other hand I may be in evening dress on my way to an important public function. These and many more may be the outer factors which in rapid succession make themselves felt and call forth reactions from my imagination. In addition to that there is my inner ' constellation ' of factors. I may be ready to sacrifice for others or, on the other hand, be of a calculating and selfish nature ; I may have an innate horror of water or a great love for it ; all these are factors helping to determine my choice.

In the fraction of a second my choice may be made, quicker in fact than it is possible for me afterwards to retrace the different eventualities conjured up in succession by my imagination. Yet, at the actual moment of choice all these combine as a ' constellation ' of physiological and psychological factors which go to determine my choice. Reading the history of the event backwards we could, if we had sufficient knowledge, trace the choice made back to the physical, emotional, mental and spiritual causes of which it was the result. Even if, at the moment of choice, a sudden inspiration or heroic enthusiasm appeared to descend upon me, sweeping aside all mundane considerations and carrying me on to an action of which normally I should not have been capable, even then it is always possible to determine what made this descent of a lofty impulse possible. It may be that the entire situation, the general conditions made, as it were, an opening through which the highest in me could manifest, it is possible that many years of thought and feeling along certain lines now culminate in an action to which they all contribute, but in each case the manifestation from on high, the inspiration or spiritual influx can be traced to causes, determining conditions, not necessarily physical, but none the less causes. Thus, even in the supreme crises of our life there is a causality which determines the result, and yet our experience of the making of the choice may be one of a wavering to and fro, a hesitation and deliberation and finally a triumphant victory over obstacles or a dismal failure and collapse. These are but, as it were, the method by which factor after factor makes itself felt and sways us emotionally or calls forth a reaction of the imagination, until finally the result is produced.

It is therefore a mistake to look upon this causality as a compelling fate from without ; the most important and decisive factors which help to determine our choice come from within : our own character, the usual trend of our thoughts and feelings, our ' inner ' life, these are determining factors in the momentous choices we have to make in life. Our natural aversion to the conception of determinism, of a preordained future, is largely due to the mistaken idea that all our actions, all our creative efforts are determined by a blind fate, compelling us from without. If we speak of compulsion we must realize that it is mainly a compulsion from within and that the determinism, in which the future is predestined, is largely a self-determinism. Even so, our innate feeling that we are free to choose will assert itself again and again.

FREEWILL AND LICENCE

One of the most confusing factors in any discussion concerning the freedom of the will is that the popular conception of such a freedom is the ability ' to do just as we like.' Freedom of the will to us means freedom to do either the one thing or the other, we are free to go out walking or to stay at home. Yet there are doubtful features about this conception of freedom.

There are only few, if any, people in these days, who are enabled by social and other conditions to do just as they like. But even if we were to imagine a tyrant, possessed of vast wealth and of perfect health, whose word was law in the community over which he reigned, without there being anyone to call him to account or punish him for his actions, then such a tyrant might be able to do as he liked, but he, no more than his meanest slave, could make a choice without determining factors. Whether, in the whim of the moment, he may decide to build a marble palace or to strike off the head of his prime minister, there must be factors to bring about his wish to do so. They may be instincts or impulses of the moment, they may be sudden ideas or the outcome of a long train of thought, but in all cases they must be determined by a constellation of physical and psychic factors. Even the choice of the tyrant is determined by influences from without and from within which can only bring about the result or the choice to which he comes and his choice is no more free than that of any other man. What is called free will in this case is but licence ; in the very actions in which he does exactly as he likes, the licentious tyrant is but a slave of his own passing desires, his likes and dislikes, and we cannot call his will free any more than that of a prisoner in his dungeons.

If our considerations of the problem of the freedom of the will are to bear any fruit we must utterly repudiate the conception of a free will as the power ' to do just as we like.' This idea of freedom is so ingrained in the average mind that it dominates all thoughts upon the matter and yet, what is here called freedom is merely the absence of outer or physical hindrances in the carrying out of our desire of the moment. It is true, nothing can prevent the tyrant from carrying out his will, but that does not make his *will* any more free than that of any other human being, it merely makes the execution of his wishes unhindered. When we decide, or choose, the absence of physical hindrances no more makes us free than the absence of material obstacles makes free the flight of a bullet ; it is determined in its flight whether it hits anything or not. Even so our behaviour is determined by factors from within and from without, whether in the carrying out of our decision we meet with obstacles or not. The average mind is so essentially unphilosophical in its approach to all problems that we must truly clean out an Augean stable of confusions before even an approach to the question is possible.

It is well then to consider first what we mean by the very term free will. When can we call the will free ? Surely only that is free which has no limitation, which is not determined or even influenced by anything else, and can we say that ever of our will ? Our will, at least in its manifestations in our daily existence, is ever determined by physiological and psychic factors. How then can we call it free ? If freedom is absence of limitation and of determination from without, only that can be free besides which naught else exists and is there any human will of which we can say that ? In this sense of the word freedom, and philosophically we cannot well take it in any other sense, only the Absolute is free, the relative is ever determined by its very relations in the world of relativity. There is no freedom in the world of the relative and to speak of a free will, to search for a freedom of the will in that world of relativity is as impossible as the quadrature of the circle. The phrase freedom of the will is a contradiction in terms ; no will can be free in the world of relativity.

We are thus once again confronted by a problem born of illusion, a question which in itself is wrong. The free will for which we seek as the ability to do exactly as we like, to do either this *or* that, is but a scarcely veiled necessity, determined from within by factors present in our consciousness which we do not recognize as compelling influences, but vaguely associate with our inner life. Yet our desires and passions, our habits of thought and feeling, our customary ways of acting are determining influences in all our choices and make the very term ' freedom ' a misnomer. When we assert the freedom of our human will we assert about that will something that can never be claimed for anything in the world of the relative.

Our question is wrong because it is the result of two illusions, that of an objective, absolute time with a future that is not yet and a past that is no more, and secondly our illusion of being a separate individual self without relation to the rest of the universe. Time with its structure of past, present and future is the product of our externalized world-image ; we objectivate that time and believe it to be an external reality. In that illusion of an absolute, external time the past is fixed for ever and the future is as yet uncertain, and it is only in that illusion that the problem of the freedom of the will can flourish. The conception of a free will is ever associated with the conception of being able to choose or decide one way *or* another, that is to say, it presupposes a future which is not yet there, but which can be shaped by our decisions. Since, however, that objectivated time is an illusion we cannot hope to solve a problem born of it ; we must withdraw from the entanglements of our world-image and enter the world of Reality where alone we can know things as they are.

THE PROBLEM IN THE WORLD OF THE REAL

Once again we must abandon the realm of illusion in which our many wrong problems originate and enter the world of Reality where alone truth can be experienced. It is only when we withdraw from the illusions of our world-image and pass through our centre of consciousness into the world of Reality that we realize how distorted the problem of the freedom of the will really is, what a contradiction in terms it contains and how impossible it is even to attempt a solution.

When we escape from the tyranny of our time-illusion with its uncertain future and experience eternal Reality we realize how much the problem of the freedom of our will is bound up with our usual concept of time. In that illusion the thought can live that somehow we can choose one way or another, that we by our God-given free will can determine the future according to our choice. But when we enter the world of Reality we experience time as an eternal Present and the very thought of a past which is done with and a future which is not yet becomes absurd. As well might the wanderer along the road think of the road behind him as fixed and certain because he, the wanderer has passed over it, and of the road in front of him as indeterminate and uncertain because he himself has not yet reached it.

The gradual evolution, growth and change which we experience in our lives is but our realization of that which we eternally are in the world of Reality. In that world the life-cycle of any creature or thing is a complete being and we look in vain for distinction of past and future. That distinction exists only for us and it is caused by our realization, it does not exist as such in the world of the Real. Thus what we call the future is fully and really present in this world of the Eternal Now as well as the past, and there is no more uncertainty about that which we have not yet experienced in the illusion of our world-image as there is about that which we have experienced. In that world of reality I am, even now, all that in my world-image I shall be in the future, and I am all this not in a vague outline, in principle, but in every detail which shall be.

Sometimes a view is propounded which attempts to strike a happy mean between determinism and free will and which says that, of course, the future is determined in large outline, that it is certain that definite great events must be accomplished, but that within these great outlines there is room for our human wills to move about, that within those limits we can choose freely how to act. It then depends on the strenuous nature of our endeavours how soon the great events which have to come can be realized, we can quicken or retard evolution, but never finally oppose it. A plausible doctrine this, but a philosophical impossibility. When once we have realized the nature of time and experienced Reality as *eternal* we can no longer make compromises in which a little eternity is mixed with a little time. We cannot mix illusion and reality ; in the world of the Real there is no question of wide and vague outlines within which the individual artist can fill in his own patterns ; in the world of the Real we are all we ever shall be.

Our time-experience is but a realization of eternity and the history of our lives is caused by that which we *are* in the world of the Eternal. We cannot look upon the events of our lives as *additions* which we constantly make to Reality. As well might we think of the spectator at a moving-picture show as causing the next picture or event upon the screen by his presence, by his perception of the picture shown. What we are in the world of Reality is no more determined by our daily actions and experience than the picture is determined by the spectator. Yet in this case we are spectator, picture and screen all in one ; when the history of our lives is unrolled we experience what we ourselves are in the world of the Real.

It is part of our illusion that we should think of our actions as they appear in our world-image, as producing reality. All that to us appears as action, creation, doing or thinking is but our realization of That which is. In that realization eternal Reality appears as an endless chain of cause and effect ; one event appears to *produce* the next event, whereas in the world of the Real all events are but part of unchanging Reality. Thus our struggles, our failures and victories, our hesitation and our choice are one and all our realization of that which we eternally are in the world of the Real.

Once we have conquered the illusion of an objective time, once we have realized the Eternal and know, beyond the shadow of a doubt, that It is the only Reality, the only World that is, the question of the freedom of the human will becomes impossible, at least in the form in which it usually is presented. The future is now, as much as the past is now, and nothing can change that future any more than anything can change the past. Past and future are but names we give to our experience of a Reality which is unchanging, and unless that central fact becomes more to us than an intellectual theory, becomes realization, we cannot hope ever to transcend the problem of the freedom of the will. We must conquer illusion before we can know Reality.

In the world of the Real we not only transcend the illusion of an objective time, we also transcend the illusion of being a separate self over against a world which is not-self. It is true, there are some who are so attached to the duality of self and not-self that they would transfer it even into the world of Reality. Sooner, however, could a miser take his hoard of gold with him through the gateway of death than that we can take with us our dearly beloved illusions through the portal of Reality. There is no self or not-self in the world of the Real, there is only That which we ourselves become in the supreme Experience. When, in the light of that experience we consider the question of the freedom of the will we can see how distorted it is, how impossible, from the standpoint of all embracing Unity.

When we inquire into the freedom of the will we speak of the will of a supposedly separate human being ; we want to know whether *our* will is free. But *our* will is a relative fact. We fondly imagine ourselves to be separate creatures, sharply distinct from the world which we are not, from our fellowmen who are different creatures. In the world of Reality, however, this illusion is no more. We are all things and a separate will becomes an impossible conception. We can now see how in our original question a number of illusions converged ; we asked for freedom for the individual will when there is no such thing as a separate being, we asked for freedom in the world of the relative when the very fact of relativity precludes freedom, we asked for the ability to choose one way or another when the future is as eternally real as the past, we asked for impossibilities which an ingenious intellect may succeed in proving to be possible, but which remain—creatures of illusion.

MISINTERPRETATIONS BY THE INTELLECT

Since the intellect is the mind functioning within the illusions of the world-image its questions and problems are always born of illusion and wrong in themselves, and the reality of things will always be unintelligible to it. When we attempt to describe the reality of things the intellect will either turn away in disgust, accusing us of evading the question, or else it will interpret in its way the reality of which we speak, and inevitably land in misconceptions. It is the curse of the intellect that it always thinks in duality and cannot know unity or synthesis. When we say that our apparent evolution is but a realization of that which we are in eternal Reality the intellect interprets this as if we were but passive spectators or instruments in a process which we cannot influence, but which determines us and our future. Determinism, to the intellect, is always a determination of our future *by something else*, whereas what takes place is self-realization, we realize that which we are and are determined by our own eternal being.

When we say that we cannot choose one way or another because the future is a present reality even now, as definitely real as what we call the past, the interpretation of this truth by the intellect becomes the doctrine of an irresistible fate which, with a grim and ruthless determination, forces us into the mould of a future from which there is no escape.

The intellect always objectivates and externalizes that which is within, and when it attempts to interpret reality it ever commits the unpardonable sin of trying to make the reality of things fit into the illusions and distortions of the world-image to which it, the intellect, is bound. Then, in its pitiable pride, it imagines that it has proved reality to be wrong or self-contradictory, whereas it has but proved its own inadequacy to approach reality or to interpret it.

This is the reason why the facts of reality are dangerous to the intellect ; in its misconceptions and its inability to see more than one aspect of the truth it is apt to be led astray by the little it understands and come to grief through its errors. Thus it will say ' if all that is to come is determined even now, why should man strive, why not sit down and do nothing ? ' Why not, indeed—if he can. Let him but try, and ere long hunger and thirst, desire and yearning will cause him to act, will drive him into action. Even the action of the Indian fakir, who sits down and refuses to move again, living a life resembling death, is but his realization in time, in the world of the relative, of a phase of his own eternal being in the world of Reality. Our illusion of having cheated fate by doing nothing at all is in itself determined by factors in our character or circumstances which could not produce any other result, and our life of idleness, if we choose to live it, would in itself be a necessity, our experience of an ever-present reality in the world of the true Being. We cannot cheat fate because what we call fate is our own eternal reality ; whatever we do, whatever we say or think is by our action or thinking proved to be part of our eternal reality ; our action or speech is but our realization of that which we are.

Again the intellect will say ; ' What about striving and struggling ? What about our endeavours to live a spiritual life, our successes and failures ? Why strive if our achieve ments are but illusion ? ' We should indeed be wrong if we said that they were illusion and equally wrong if we said they were not. The illusory part is that, while the issue seems uncertain, we think it may fall out one way *or* another, reality is that what we experience as effort and struggle in our world-image is in very truth part of our real being in the world of the Eternal, a part which we in our world-image interpret as ' struggle,' ' endeavour ' or ' effort.' The supreme effort in which we strain every fibre of our being to achieve a certain end is our interpretation of a phase of our real being, as important and essential a part of our eternal cycle of life, as any part could be, but we err when we think the outcome is uncertain.

While we live in the illusions of our world-image we are limited by them and have to acknowledge the relative reality of time. Though I may know that, in the world of the Real, all time, past and future, is an ever-present reality, I have to submit to the time of my world-image, when I want to be in time for a train, when I am dealing with my world-image interpretation of things as they are ; I must acknowledge time in its illusions, even while I know reality. The wise philosopher is not he who, having seen the vision of Reality, attempts to force this upon his world-image, but he who, having experienced Reality and knowing it within himself, is able to recognize the limitations and illusions of his world-image consciousness and act accordingly.

Our striving to attain some noble end is not all illusion ; it is interpretation of reality, part of our self-realization. To conclude that, because all things past and future are an ever-present reality, all striving and effort are unnecessary and vain and may well be abandoned, would be as foolish as it would be to abstain from choosing any food because we know that our apparent freedom of choice is but illusion : the result would be starvation. He who would live according to the world of the Real in the illusion of his world-image can only end his days in a lunatic asylum; he would be attempting that which cannot and should not be attempted. The interpretation of reality which we see in our world-image, is not the same as reality itself; the features of reality appear in a strange and distorted way in our world-image and we must not commit the philosophical mistake of thinking that we can transfer bodily the conditions of the world of the Real into our world-image. Could we do that it would no longer be our world-image, but the world of the Real. The Absolute can never be contained in the relative, yet he who has realized the Absolute will, living in the world of the relative, find his experience to be as a shining light illumining his way and giving peace in the midst of chaos and turmoil. But never can he dream of attempting to transfer ultimate Reality bodily into the world of the relative.

Such is the answer to those who would misinterpret the fact that in the world of the Real the future is even now present, and find in that a reason for the cessation of effort. Not in this way does the Vision on the Mount illumine our life in the valley; its lesson is not that we can now cease from effort since ' all is fixed anyhow,' but rather that in all our effort, in all our struggles we henceforth feel the Peace of the Eternal. Success and failure, misfortune or good luck become to us matters not to be grieved over or rejoiced in; one and all they are recognized as our eternal Being; however intense our effort may have been, once the outcome is definite to us in our illusion of time, we recognize and know that nothing else could have been, and we are at peace. Thus our vision of reality bestows a serenity on our life, an absence of anxiety and worry which is as the radiance of the Eternal shining in the uncertainty of time.

THE REALITY OF FREEDOM

The question now remains, what of freedom? The conviction that somehow freedom is the consummation of life, the identification of our highest spiritual state with freedom, is so persistent that, even though we may recognize that the freedom for which the man in the street clamours is but ill-disguised licence, we yet feel that there must be true freedom somewhere and that in some way it must be the expression of the highest we can attain.

There is indeed freedom. When we enter the world of the Real we do experience freedom, not the illusion of freedom which was 'to do as we liked,' to have our own way, to choose without compulsion, but a true Freedom in which we are free because there is nothing outside us to limit or compel. As long in the illusion of our world-image we imagined ourselves to be separate individuals with a will of our own, surrounded by a world full of opposition and of other creatures with wills of their own, our demand for freedom was as impossible as would be the demand of a swimmer that the water should not wet him. In our very assertion of individuality, in our separateness we are unfree, since we are limited by all that which we are not, influenced, opposed and compelled by the surroundings in which we live, by the character with which we identify ourselves. Our very physical existence makes us unfree, we are bound in one place and can only move about on the face of the earth by the aid of complicated technical means. When a man says 'I am free' his very assertion is a contradiction, since 'I' can never be free and Freedom comes only when 'I' is no longer. It comes in the world of Reality when we are indeed no longer the separate creature, the individual separate from a surrounding world, but when we are That which is all things past and present. In That we are free.

Nothing now can limit or compel. We are the road on which we walk as well as the man we meet and the stream we have to cross. When suffering or misfortune comes to us we still are free, since we are that which hurts us as well as the one who took that which was ours. Here then is freedom, when Nature by her laws no longer limits or compels us, when we are Nature and her laws our will, when man no more opposes or restrains our will, since we are all men. The phantom freedom, for which we so loudly clamoured when we were bound in illusion, now seems a paltry and a petty thing, impossible and full of contradictions. In the joy of our true Freedom, we no longer need it, since we are That which contains it and infinitely more. Who would desire a thing when he is all things, and what greater freedom can there be than that which becomes ours when we are ultimate Reality, beyond which and outside which nothing is ? Then are freedom and necessity seen as one, necessity the way in which freedom appears to man, bound in illusion.

Knowing that Freedom we are invincible. Nature in the strength of her elements may oppose us, man in his violence imprison and humiliate us, all we have may be taken from us and yet we shall be rich beyond imagination, being all things, and live in utter freedom, since we are prison as well as prisoner. Our will is free when it no more desires to do this or the other thing, but when it knows that whatever happens is its own expression. Such is the Freedom of the Will.

PARTIAL VIEWS

If we were asked whether this conception of necessity and free will which we gain in the world of reality agrees with either the doctrine of determinism or with that which upholds the freedom of the will we should find it difficult to give an answer, since under these terms such very different things may be understood.

There is a determinism which is materialistic and mechanical, in which living man is ignored, in which creative effort is ruled out and all is made part of a mechanical chain of cause and effect. Here man is conceived to be determined even as the reactions in the laboratory of the scientist are determined and can be calculated. In such a determinism indeed there is no place for creative effort, no place for vision or inspiration, man is levelled down to a merely physical event. But man is more than that ; he is an emotional, mental and spiritual being as well as a physical one, the factors which determine his choices in life are factors of emotion, of mind and spirit as well as physical influences. In the theory of materialistic determinism the real, inner, creative man is ignored ; determinism here is but a ruthless fate, compelling man from without.

Some, on the other hand, who teach the freedom of the will present this, as if in the midst of the physical chain of cause and effect there take place irruptions from within through which man in his freedom is creatively manifest. Such psychic irruptions, like the actions of a *deus ex machina*, are then not causally determined, but are looked upon as spontaneous and unaccountable ; our freedom is considered to be an activity, entirely undetermined by anything from within or from without. There is, however, a causality of psychic events as well as a causality of physical events, the inspiration of the poet, the dream of the social reformer or the vision of the saint, however far removed they may be from mere physical happenings, are yet causally connected with preceding events, and even their irruptions into the physical realm are made possible only by certain conditions which provide the necessary opening. With regard to this physical world they certainly are creative, they mould and determine ; in their creative activity, however, they are causally connected with other events and psychically or spiritually determined.

We hold then, with the determinist, that the future is determined, we differ from him in that we look upon that determination, not as coming from without and being of a material nature, but as the realization, in the illusion of time, of ever-present Reality. Determinism in man's life thus becomes self-realization ; man's future is predestined by that which he himself is in the world of the Real.

We hold with those who teach the freedom of the will that man's greatness is his creative power which, from the world within, can and does mould the physical world ; we, however, do not look upon this creative activity as causeless and unaccountable, but as determined from within by spiritual, mental or emotional facts.

Finally and above all we look upon the Freedom of the Will not as the power to do as we like, to do one thing *or* another, but as the supreme glory of that realization in which we know ourselves as all that is. In that unity we are free, in that Freedom necessity itself is but the expression of our own being.

CHAPTER NINE

THE JUSTICE OF LIFE

Our being thus, from threshold unto threshold throughout the realm, is a joy to all the realm as to the King, who draweth our wills to what he willeth.—DANTE, *Paradiso.*

THE PROBLEM OF INJUSTICE

ALL men expect justice from life but few there are that find it. The reward of the virtuous and the punishment of the wicked may have their place in novel and melodrama and perhaps explain their popularity, but the bare facts of daily life appear to show the opposite—the meek and gentle perish, the ruthless flourish. Can we wonder that many a man, not conscious of wrong-doing and yet deprived of the labours of his years and of all that he holds dear, cries out in agony that there is no justice in life and that, if there is a God this God cannot be a just One ?

It is but a meagre consolation, inspired by our desires rather than by scientific observation, that the rewards and punishments, which are so obviously absent in life down here, should materialize in a hereafter where the just play harps in bliss and the wicked feed the fires of hell. It is but a second line of defence in which our wish for justice in life entrenches itself and where, seeing itself defeated by the facts of daily existence, it fights for the fulfilment of its hopes, in a hereafter, the conditions of which few can test or deny.

There is no doubt that life appears to deal out with a

sublime indifference joy or suffering, happiness or misfortune to the good and the wicked alike ; with impartiality the darts and arrows of an outrageous fortune appear to be scattered over this world, with an entire unconcern for the hapless individual who chances to be in their way. Do we not know only too many instances of brave and patient workers who never appear to receive the reward of their toil, and from whom even the little that they had is taken away ? And how often is not success or power but the result of a ruthlessness which, regardless of ruin to others, carves its way through life and attains its end though it brings suffering to millions ?

The great are but too often the ruthless ; where the man endowed with imagination and compassion would shrink back from an action that would bring profit and power to himself but misery to others, the one who lacks this quality of sympathetic imagination will not be deterred by the sufferings of his fellowmen if he but attains his end. And when these ends have been attained humanity, in its adoration of power and success, is but too willing to forget the way by which they were achieved or maintained and sees but the dazzling height on which the successful man has enthroned himself. The meek may inherit heaven, they certainly do not inherit the earth ; the more a follower of Christ endeavours to tread in the footsteps of his Master the more he shall find himself deprived of power and possessions, scorned by man as a failure and trodden underfoot by the successful and the great.

Must we then surrender and put by the justice of life with many an old myth or fancy in the lumber room of exploded superstitions, or is it possible that philosophy will hold out another hope for that which is so dear to most of us ?

It would be well if, from time to time, when we contemplate the problem of the justice of life, we asked ourselves what we consider to be the things worth striving for and

worth attaining, what we consider the highest reward in life
and what the greatest evil that can overtake a man. It is
clear that unless it is understood what we are to consider a
good thing or an evil thing in life we cannot judge whether
there is justice or not, since justice depends on the reward
for good deeds done and the punishment for evil ones.
Now it is surely no exaggeration to say that in the minds of
the majority of Christian men and women reward, or the good
things of life, consist in money, power and pleasure, evil in
obscurity, loss and suffering.

There is no fault to be found with this appreciation of
values in life ; every human being, according to his nature
and mentality, must have a sense of values expressing his
level in evolution. But when nations call themselves with
pride Christian nations, when we not only laud and praise
the divine wisdom of Christ, but even demand that other
nations and races too shall acknowledge him as Wisdom
incarnate, then surely we should at least grant some measure
of reality to the scale of values of which His words bear
witness. And here we find no uncertain message ; like a
golden thread the teaching runs through the Gospel-story
that there is but one thing worth gaining in life, one supreme
value and that is the realization of the Kingdom within, the
Kingdom of God. In this realization of divinity alone can
be found peace, happiness and riches, compared to which
the wealth of the earth is of no worth.

If we claim truth for the words of Christ there is no escape
from the conclusion that reward in life can only mean a
fuller realization of the Kingdom, while punishment can
be only understood to mean estrangement from that highest
Good. Thus we have no choice ; if we desire to call ourselves
Christians and uphold the truth of Christ's teachings we
must also uphold that justice in life means that the good shall

gain a fuller realization of that which is of the greatest value :
the Kingdom of God, and that the wicked as a result of their
evil deeds shall find themselves far from that supreme
happiness. The fact that they gain many of the things of
this earth, such as power and possessions can, in the light
of Christian teaching, never be taken as a possible equivalent
or substitute for that which alone is worth having, the
realization of the Kingdom within, and on the other hand,
even if all the evils of life were poured forth upon a man and,
like Job, he were to find himself the chosen of misfortune,
even then a realization of the Kingdom within should more
than outweigh these worldly evils ; from a standpoint of
justice the man would indeed have his reward.

Too often, however, we are not Christians but only
members of Christian Churches and as such we extol to the
heights the glories of Christ's teaching and are intolerant of
the heathen who fail to embrace it, but we do not think of
applying this teaching to the problems of our lives. Our
Christianity is a frail plant which can only flower in the
hot-house of Church worship and which dies a speedy death
when brought into the cold atmosphere of our daily lives ;
on Monday morning our sense of values changes and we do
not desire the Kingdom of God, of which we sang so fervently
the day before, half as much as the increase of our business.
Then too the problem of the justice of life presents itself in
a very different light ; in church indeed we praise the
blessedness of the saints as the highest reward, but at home
we are quite willing, more than willing, to forego these rather
nebulous rewards of heaven for the more tangible rewards
of the earth ; the one bird in the hand is still worth more
to us than all the birds that ever were in the heavenly bush.

Consequently we complain that life is not just because the
man who follows in the footsteps of Christ does not get rich,

does not get honoured and famous, does not attain to high position or political power, but is far more often a failure from all social standpoints, trampled under foot in the struggle for existence. But our complaints about the injustice of life remain essentially unchristian and we can only indulge in them if at the same time we are willing, and honest enough, to express our entire disbelief in the message which Christ brought to humanity and for which He gave His life. If we cannot be Christians we can at least be sincere.

SUBSTITUTES FOR JUSTICE

The problem yet remains for the majority of men that life deals her cards in an entire indifference and disregard of persons, if anything, with a slight leaning towards the wicked. Even if our Christianity is real to us it is difficult, when we see the tyranny of evil and ignorance over the gentle and the wise, to refrain from wondering whether there is justice for the individual. There is no doubt, it leaves a feeling of dissatisfaction, of incompleteness in our minds to see the incompatibility of a man's actions with the results that seem to come to him in life ; unconsciously, if not consciously, we all desire to see life complete, balanced, the good rewarded and happy, the evil punished and miserable.

A novel or drama with an incomplete, unhappy ending is hardly ever popular ; even if life cheats us out of reward and punishment we can at least demand them from fiction, and much of the gratification we gain from the stories we read, or see on stage and screen, is derived from the fact that here at least things happen as they should—the hero is rewarded, the villain defeated. Our starved sense of justice comes to life again under such circumstances and when, from the reading or the contemplation of such soul-satisfying dramas, we return to our daily lives, we cannot help but see how lacking they are in logic and reason. But then life is neither logical nor reasonable.

Another substituted remedy for our dissatisfaction with life's dealings lies in our conceptions of a life after death. Even if the good does not receive the reward of his actions in this life then surely he must get it after death, there if not here will he receive the bliss which is his by rights. Let the wicked rejoice in their ill-gotten gains in the brief span of life that is theirs, soon the time will come that amidst gnashing of teeth and bitter tears they suffer the just retribution for their evil deeds. Then, from the everlasting bliss of heaven, the good can smile down in a divine complacency on the everlasting torments of the damned ; yes, in the strange mentality of some it would even seem as if the life of blessedness gained an additional flavour from the contemplation of sufferings which have no end.

From a psychological standpoint the joys of heaven and the sufferings of hell are but a substitute for that justice which we do not find in daily life ; in the life after death the incomplete fragments of life are supplemented and made complete by the reward or punishment lacking here.

Even the nature of the infernal torments and the celestial joys is a product of our earthly desires and fears ; the hell of the northern peoples is as cold as the hell thought out in the tropics is hot. In a similar manner the activities in man's celestial home change with the fashions of the ages ; for the Egyptian rich wheatfields and harvests produced without labour, for the Red Indian the happy hunting grounds with plentitude of game and unending sport, for our Teutonic forefathers Walhalla with plenty of fighting and beer drunk from the skulls of former enemies, the Mohammedan's paradise is resplendent with houris and who can think of a Christian heaven without harps and everlasting hymns of praise ?

No, even our nebulous beliefs that somehow after death all will come right, cannot solve our problem of the injustice of life ; it is too patently man's own creation. Also the just-wait-and-see-what-happens-to-you-when-you-are-dead attitude hardly gives us that justice which we desire to see *now* in life ; it is a very meagre consolation for the victim to know that after death the one who robbed him will suffer untold agonies while he himself is bathed in a self-righteous bliss. If man is to believe in the justice of life he must have ' grounds more relative than this.'

THE DOCTRINE OF KARMA AND THE JUSTICE OF LIFE

It is inevitable that the life of man on earth should be unintelligible as long as it is considered by itself instead of as part of the great cycle of life which every individual being accomplishes from beginning to end. We all complete the creative Rhythm in our own evolution ; we all grow from the unconscious unity of primitive man through the separateness of intellectual man to the conscious unity of spiritual man ; we all grow from the savage to the saint in our pilgrimage through these worlds of matter. In one single life we appear but to advance a step on this long path towards perfection and we cannot avoid the conclusion that it is through many lives on earth that we complete our cycle of evolution.

When thus we see one life in its causal connection with lives preceding and following it, we realize the utter impossibility of finding the justice, for which we seek, realized in a period not complete in itself. As well might we consider one single day in our life and demand to see that day a complete whole, balanced within its own limits ; every day of necessity continues the work of previous days ; we wake up with the results of the actions we did the day before or earlier yet ; we continue the relations with our fellowmen which we began previously, and our whole day's work is inextricably bound up with the work of previous days. The same interconnection exists between the days of our greater life, each of which is one life on earth ; it is our action in one life which produces results not only in that same life, but in lives to come. The ties for good or evil, which we make in any one life with our fellowmen and which at the end of such a life are but too often left incomplete and unadjusted, will be taken up in some next life when once again we meet those whom we have wronged or helped. How else could our evolution be a continuous one if there were not this causal connection between our different lives on earth ; each life being both the harvest of previous ones and in its actions the seed for a harvest in lives to come ?

Here then appears a new hope for justice in life ; if man's successive lives on earth are all causally connected then the circumstances in which he finds himself born in some particular life, the advantages or disadvantages, the good or ill fortune, which come to him, however unjust they may appear, must necessarily be connected with and caused by the events of his previous lives. The explanation of the apparent injustices of life is then that the misfortune of one man and the good fortune of another are the result of their own respective actions in the past, the just consequence of their own behaviour. We can hardly look upon them as rewards or punishments since the lives of man are bound together in a chain of cause and effect and in that causality it is as inevitable that actions bring their own results as it is with regard to physical happenings. The law of cause and effect takes the place of a God who deals out rewards and punishments ; if we offend against the law the result must inevitably follow. It does not help to say that we did not know the law or that we are sorry for what we did ; he who holds his hand in the fire must of necessity burn his fingers, whether he knew that fire is hot or not.

According to this doctrine of *karma*, as it is called in Hindu and Buddhist philosophy, we at the same time undergo the effects of our past actions and by our actions now cause the conditions of our future existence ; our entire evolution is one connected whole. The apparent injustices of social life now become intelligible ; the man who in past lives has ever tried to benefit his fellowmen will be born in circumstances and with possibilities which will give him a wider scope for his powers for good, he who did but seek himself and brought evil to others will be born in conditions where through suffering he will learn the inviolable unity of life.

Is then the problem of the injustice of life at last solved ? Can we at last say that life is just, since the law of cause and effect works with never-failing exactitude ? We certainly have seen how the events and circumstances of one life are connected with previous ones, but even so the question remains, what causes the difference between the cycle of evolution of one individual and that of another. The evolution of no two human beings is the same and the very fact of their difference shows an inherent inequality. Justice demands equality, inequality suggests injustice and the question remains, why are the paths which human beings go in their evolutionary cycles so very different ?

If we trace this inequality to its beginning we must mark as such the moment when the individual emerges from the group-life of nature, when from the group-life, which dominated animal existence, there is born the individual human being. This moment of *individualization* marks the beginning of the human cycle of evolution and, since this moment must of necessity be different for all human beings their evolutionary cycles must be different too.

In theosophical literature it is explained that the individualization of the animal from the group-life to which it belonged, takes place only in the case of domestic animals and that it is their close contact with man and their response to human qualities of emotion or mind which causes the actual birth of the individual from the group-life of the animal species. When the animal is thus ' individualized ' its next appearance on earth will be as a human being ; the beginning of its human cycle of evolution is marked by that especial response of the domestic animal which causes it to individualize. It is further taught that there are different ways or modes of individualization ; the animal may be born as a human being through love, wisdom or devotion, the so-called *right* modes of individualization, and also through fear, hatred, or pride, the so-called *wrong* modes of individualization. It is described in several theosophical works how this mode of individualization affects the entire evolutionary cycle of the human being who thus emerges from the animal kingdom. If the individualization takes place through love and devotion the path of evolution will be smooth and harmonious, joyful and constructive. If, however, individualization takes place through hatred or fear, caused generally by human cruelty to the animal, then the entire evolutionary cycles of the unfortunate human beings who thus emerged into individuality are branded with all the vices and attendant miseries to be found in human life ; their evolution is retarded, they suffer untold agonies in their constant rebellion against their spiritual superiors, they develop into heartless oppressors of their fellowmen, thus making even more evil ' karma ' which will bring yet more suffering ; in short, they seem to evolve through evil-doing and through suffering. Yet it is clear that the animal cannot help its mode of individualization and that the individual

who thus emerges from the animal species is not responsible
for the treatment which the human beings in charge of those
animals have given them.   Yet as an individual he has to
suffer all the miseries and misfortunes of a wrong mode of
individualization, life after life.   Where then is justice ?

The law of karma does indeed show us how different lives
are interconnected, how the events of one life produce the
circumstances of the next, as such it explains much and is
*a most valuable addition to our knowledge of the method of
evolution.*   What, however, it does not and cannot explain
is *why* some human beings should be born as individuals in
a way which brands them as evil and rebellious for their
whole further evolution, whereas others should have the
apparently unfair privilege of individualizing in the right
way and evolving along lives of harmony and joy.   The
problem of justice therefore is not solved by the doctrine of
karma which does but teach the causal connection between
successive lives ; the problem has only been shifted back to
the beginning of human evolution and the inequality between
one man's evolution and another's still remains unexplained.

So often we think that we have solved a problem when we
have restated it in unusual terminology or else have shifted
it back a few hundred thousand years.   However valuable
the doctrines of reincarnation and karma are we must
recognize that fundamentally and ultimately they do not
solve the question of the justice of life.   That question is of
a different order altogether and we damage rather than
enhance the nobility of the doctrines mentioned when we
try to make them serve as solutions for problems which
belong to the domain of ultimate Reality.   The doctrines of
reincarnation and karma belong to the world of relativity ;
their value and teaching is scientific, not philosophical.   From
the philosophical standpoint it matters little indeed whether

the inequality in man's lives is caused by the arbitrary decision of a Deity who places each soul in different circumstances, or whether it is caused by the difference in modes of individualization from the animal kingdom ; the problem of injustice remains.

It is difficult for many to see whether an answer really solves a problem or whether it merely restates it or shifts it back, and it would be a useful work to show in religion, philosophy and science the many instances where an explanation of the *method*, or the way in which events take place, is accepted as a solution or explanation of the fundamental and ultimate *reason* of the entire process. The doctrines of reincarnation and karma give a most valuable exposition of the *process* of individual evolution in our world, as such the doctrines are true and of the utmost importance, but they do not finally solve the problem of the apparent injustice of life. That problem still demands a solution.

THE ERRONEOUS NATURE OF THE PROBLEM

Once again we must analyze the problem itself and see whether or not there is an element of error in it which may make it incapable of being solved.

Let us then consider the problem of justice and see whether it is right in itself. Man, seeing the inequality of circumstances and fortunes in this world, demands some form of compensation which will finally make every one's portion of good and evil equal to that of all others. This, put somewhat crudely, is the fundamental demand behind the question of the justice of life for the individual.

A certain pettiness underlies such clamouring for justice ; we would fain see the Deity seated on His throne above, portioning out the delicacies and woes of life with an impartiality and an unfailing correctness of weight and measure of which a village grocer might be proud, and we follow with jealous eyes the portions which our fellowmen receive, comparing them surreptitiously to our own and measuring them off one against the other so as to make quite sure that all are equal. Is that a mentality from which a philosophical question, let alone a philosophical answer, can ever be produced? And even if the question were not essentially wrong is our concern over it compatible with human dignity?

Apart, however, from the not very exalted level of thought which produces the problem, and notwithstanding the controversy there has been over it throughout the ages, the question itself is impossible. The demand for justice is ultimately the demand that each separate human being shall get an equal deal from life and that the sum total of joy and of pain shall be more or less the same for all. The problem therefore is based on the conception of ourselves as separate individuals, detached from all others and living a life of our own, self-contained, with its end and purpose in itself; only in this conception of a separate individuality can the problem of justice have any meaning. But this sense of separateness is a basic illusion, truly inevitable in our cycle of evolution, just as the exteriorization of our world-image is inevitable, but none the less an illusion. In our everyday consciousness, permeated as it is by illusion, we feel ourselves sharply and distinctly separate from our fellow-creatures and in this feeling of separateness we produce problems which we cannot ever solve.

Such a problem is that of the justice of life, of the justice or injustice of the Deity who is supposed to be responsible for all of us and who, in our minds, should give each one of us an equally fair treatment. The problem is rooted in a sense of separateness which is illusion, consequently we can ponder over it for many centuries, but we shall never find a solution.

If we would know reality we must overcome the illusions in the problems which our intellect presents, instead of accepting them without suspicion. Thus alone can we come to living knowledge.

JUSTICE IN THE WORLD OF THE REAL

Let us then once again withdraw from the illusion of our world-image with its hosts of errors and misconceptions and enter that world of Reality where, in silence and peace, we can know things as they are, where we can experience the reality which is so vainly sought in this problem of justice. Where, in the world of relativity, the separate individual is the outstanding reality, the opposite is experienced in the world of the Real. There the outstanding and overwhelming experience is the fundamental *unity* of all that is and in that unity the multitude of creatures and things appear as notes in a vast musical composition. We ourselves are lost in the unity of the whole and in the light of that experience our normal sense of separateness looks absurd and pitiable.

Unity in the world of the Real is such a very different thing from even our highest conceptions of unity in daily life. Here we always think of unity as a combination of things which are separate ; in the world of the Real we realize that unity is not union ; the multitude of separate things no more combine to make up unity than the fractions contained within the number one produce the unity of that number by being added together. Unity is a fundamentally real thing ; multiplicity is but a way of contemplating and experiencing that unity.

When we enter the world of the Real we no longer persist as individuals, surrounded by a world which we are not ; we are all that is and our individuality seems to have merged in the All. In the world of Reality we thus live in and through everything, we *are* everything; and our dearly beloved illusion of a separate individuality, distinct from all other individualities, appears but a pitiable distortion, a terrible misconception. In the world of Reality the demand of justice for the individual is almost repulsive, it is so utterly impossible and incompatible with things as they are. In the blindness and illusion of our world-image we may fancy ourselves to be separate and distinct, yet, all the time, the fact remains that we never are separate, but are fundamentally and essentially one in being and reality. In that reality we not only share, we *are* the life of all creatures in a fullness of utter unity which is incomprehensible to our consciousness in daily life. The demand for justice is therefore meaningless in that world; it does not matter whether a thing happens to that part of reality which I call myself or to the part which I call someone else, all are one in utter unity; what happens to someone else happens to ourselves, there is but one Reality in which and through which all happens.

All things that are express the Absolute and, though the expression in relativity is in countless modes or creatures, it is but one Reality that is so expressed; unity and multiplicity are but different ways of experiencing the same reality. The manifold and apparently separate manifestations in the world of the relative are as the many separate notes out of which a great symphony is built up; there is necessarily difference between the notes and they are grouped differently into chords and harmonies, yet the symphony is one. How absurd would be the suggestion of injustice in the difference in place allotted to the different notes, in the fact that one note may form part of a majestic opening chord whereas another note is almost lost in a minor passage. The symphony is one and we cannot attribute separateness to the single notes or chords; they all are the symphony and the symphony is one.

Each note has its meaning only as part of the symphony ; the symphony is not a collection of notes grouped together into a unity, but every note is part of the symphony. The composition as a whole is the fundamental reality ; understanding that we can say that there is no such thing as a separate note in that unity ; every note shares the beauty of the whole and shares the life of every other note : the life of the symphony.

Thus are we one ; the rich variety in the world of the relative, the many apparently separate creatures and objects are but the notes and chords of the eternal Symphony of creation. No note can possibly be spared in that Symphony, no note has a separate existence, the life of the whole is in each one of them and each one shares the life, the joys and the sufferings of all the others. The demand for equality or for justice for the individual shows but that our individual note has not yet realized itself as part of the Symphony, and hears only its own meaningless sound reverberating through the void of illusion. What a difference when we realize that we are the Symphony, the Hymn of creation ; we then know that we give meaning to all other notes just as they give meaning to us, that there are no separate notes, but that all are eternally and inseparably part of the eternal Song of Life.

When we have once realized unity in the world of the Real and have seen what a distorted view the illusion of separate individuality really is we no longer ask for justice or for equality. However miserable our own individual fate may seem to be and however glorious that of another we know that we share the life of all and that, in the unity of all, our sorrow is as essentially part of the Song of creation as the joy of our neighbour. What happens to him happens to us, our fate is his fate, what we do to him is done to ourselves, what he does to us he does unto himself. In the Vision of

Reality we gain detachment from our own particular fate and circumstances ; living as we do in the unity of all things in the world of the Real we can no longer see any individual destiny as separate in its misery or joy, since we are all things simultaneously. We are the hand that strikes us and the hand that blesses, we are the multitude of living things, the whole world around us, as well as the world within. Where now is our demand for justice, what meaning has justice for us when we realize unity ? The very desire to have exactly the same as our neighbour has become absurd since we know that we are that neighbour as well as that which he receives.

It is this realization of unity of which Dante sings in the third Canto of the *Paradiso*. Here the poet meets the spirits whose eternal place in heaven is represented by the realm of the Moon, a lower cosmic sphere where those live who, in the religious life, have been prevented from keeping their vows inviolate. Thus Piccarda, with whom Dante enters into conversation, says :

> And this lot, which seemeth so far down,
> Therefore is given us because our vows were slighted,
> And on some certain side were not filled in.

Dante wonders whether these spirits do not yearn for the higher realms of Paradise, implying that they might be discontented with their lot, or envy those who are placed nearer to the Heart of things in eternal bliss. He thus asks Piccarda :

> But tell me, ye whose blessedness is here,
> Do ye desire a more lofty place,
> To see more, or to make yourselves more dear ?

It is the earthly demand for justice, which here, in Paradise, has lost its meaning :

> With those other shades first she smiled a little,
> Then answered me so joyous
> That she seemed to burn in love's first flame.

Brother, the quality of love stilleth our will,
And maketh us long only for what we have,
And giveth us no other thirst.

Did we desire to be more aloft,
Our longings were discordant from his will
Who here assorteth us,

And for that, thou wilt see, there is no room within these circles,
If of necessity we have our being here in love,
And if thou think again what is love's nature.

Nay, 'tis the essence of this blessed being
To hold ourselves within the divine will,
Whereby our own wills are themselves made one.

So that our being thus, from threshold unto threshold
Throughout the realm, is a joy to all the realm as to the king,
Who draweth our wills to what he willeth ;

And his will is our peace ;
It is that sea to which all moves
That it createth and that nature maketh.

Clear was it then to me how everywhere
In heaven is Paradise, e'en though the grace
Of the chief Good doth not rain there after one only fashion.

No words could express with more dignity or beauty the all-pervading unity of the world of the Real in which such thoughts as discontent with the place that is ours in the unity of the whole, or envy of those who are more highly placed than we, are quite impossible. It is indeed true that if we can but think what is ' love's nature ' we must see that there is no room within the realm of reality for the desire to be more aloft or for longings, discordant from the Supreme Will. Love is realization of unity and in that realization man transcends his individuality and shares the life of the whole. The being of every creature in the world of Paradise, of divine Reality, is a joy to all ' from threshold unto threshold through the realm '; the experience of each one is the experience of the whole.

As long as we are bound in the illusion of separateness we demand justice and cannot find it, when we transcend illusion and experience reality the problem of justice becomes superfluous in the very much greater truth we then have found. Thus it ever is, our problems are incapable of solution as long as we are bound to the illusion that produced them, and lose their meaning when that illusion is conquered. Solved they never are ; where solutions are claimed we can be sure that error is abroad.

It is then clear that, as Dante has it, ' everywhere in heaven is Paradise, even though the grace of the chief Good does not rain there after one only fashion.' The mystery of ultimate Reality is multiplicity in unity ; the unity is as real and eternal as is the variety of relative beings, consequently, though there must be inequality in life and fate, yet the inequality is but part of the eternal unity and can therefore never be called injustice.

In the practice of life the knowledge gained in the world of Reality means equanimity with regard to our own fate, compassion for the fate of others. Here again the intellect, in its inability to comprehend reality, will misinterpret and misunderstand that which it cannot contain. Thus it will say, ' if justice is but an illusion of the separate self there is no longer any necessity for justice in daily life ; since all are one I can treat my fellowmen badly and take all I can for myself, since my advantage is theirs too in the unity of all and their sorrow is mine. Thus I do no more wrong when I kill my neighbour in order to rob him as when I give him the best I have.' To the intellect this may seem but a logical conclusion from the experience of reality, yet it is but a distortion of truth, such as the illusion-bound intellect always makes.

The fact that in the world of the Real we share the joys

and sorrows of all creatures just as they share ours in no wise means that it therefore does not matter how we treat our fellowmen. On the contrary the only way in which we can interpret our realization of unity in the world of the relative is through love for all creatures ; just as any unkind or hurtful action is a denial of the Reality in which all are one, so are self-sacrifice, love for all that lives and service of our fellowmen the expression in the world of relativity of that supreme Reality which can never be fully expressed here, the utter unity of all that is. Love, indeed, is the nearest approach to Reality we can find in the world of the relative, in love alone does man conform to his being in the world of the Real.

Love is more than justice ; ' an eye for an eye and a tooth for a tooth ' is justice indeed, love is to forgive those that persecute us and to do good to them that hate us. The law of Moses expresses justice, the law of Christ expresses love ; *justice is the demand of those bound in the world of illusion, love the joy of those who know Reality.*

It is then true that, as long as we live in the illusion of separateness and clamour for justice, we find ourselves incapable of solving the problem of the injustice of life ; when we have transcended the illusion of separateness and have entered the world of the Real, we no longer desire to solve the problem because we see its error. Life is not concerned with the questions and errors of our illusion-bound consciousness ; *life is more than just, life is one.* In that unity of all that is, the problem of the justice of life is transcended ; the reality of the unity of life is experienced.

CHAPTER TEN

THE IMMORTALITY OF THE SOUL

The One remains, the many change and pass;
Heaven's light for ever shines, Earth's shadows fly;
Life, like a dome of many coloured glass,
Stains the white radiance of Eternity.

SHELLEY.

THE QUEST OF IMMORTALITY

AT all times man has abhorred the thought of an end to existence. It is true, humanity has ever clothed its desire to live on beyond physical death in the garments of revealed belief or philosophical truth; from the crude animism of primitive man with his spirit-belief and ancestor-worship to the measured logic of theological and philosophical argument the endeavour has always been the same—to justify the belief in a continued life after death and to eliminate the fear of an end. Yet the instinct, the desire, or even fear comes first, the justification by the intellect or by revelation afterwards; the instinct demands immortality, the intellect supplies it, complete with proof and argument.

We should ever be on our guard against doctrines which our instinctive fears and desires demand; here the investigating mind has not spontaneously discovered truth, but the *desire* for immortality has caused the intellect to furnish a doctrine of life and death that shall satisfy man's hopes and allay his fears. Of these fears the greatest, beyond question, has been and is that of death.

We love ourselves too well to be able to bear the thought that our beloved ego could ever cease to be ; rather do we accept a miserable life than no life at all. Not to be is unthinkable to us ; in the very fact of our existence now lies for us the promise and necessity of our continued existence through ages to come. Yet all appearance of the personality seems to vanish with the death of the body ; if anything does survive it escapes our perception. The evidence of our senses therefore appears to deny us that very continued existence which we desire so fervently, as strongly indeed as we fear the possibility of an end to existence with the death of the body. We feel that our lives remain incomplete, unfinished, and we conclude that there must be a life after death in which is found the balance, so sadly lacking here.

There is, however, a loftier reason for the quest of immortality ; there is in every one of us some dim perception of the fact that we are more than the body alone and that with the death of the body we do not cease to be. It is the vision of our eternal reality that inspires this conviction of immortality. Yet our intellect grasps but imperfectly what the vision means ; where the experience of reality tells of our eternal being, the interpretation by the intellect becomes a doctrine of immortality for our temporal self, in its passing appearance.

Whether our quest for immortality is inspired by this dim apprehension by the intellect of our greater being, or by the fear of our petty self which desires immortality, there is ever the demand of immortality first and the proof of it by the intellect afterwards. Thus theology and philosophy have but too often lent themselves to minister to the demand of mortal man and have but too willingly provided proofs and arguments for that which man had already decided to be necessarily true by his very fear of the terrible prospects of

the reverse. It is hardly to the credit of philosophy thus to
be ordered to find truth, with careful instructions as to where
exactly this truth will have to be found and what its
nature is to be. It is the task of philosophy to go forth
without fear or restraint and to discover things as they are,
whether they may please man's instinctive fears and desires
or not. To provide logical argumentation for a doctrine,
solely because it would be such a terrible thing if that doctrine
were not true, is as unworthy as it is unproductive of living
truth.

Thus even the arguments for immortality of Kant in his
Critique of Practical Reason are, when we come to analyze
them, but a *petitio principii*. He argues that holiness or the
perfect accordance of the will with the moral law demands
an endless progress and that ' this endless progress is only
possible on the supposition of an endless duration of the
existence and personality of the same rational being . . . the
summum bonum, then, practically is only possible on the
supposition of the immortality of the soul ; consequently
this immortality, being inseparably connected with the moral
law, is a postulate of pure practical reason.' This is not a
philosophical argumentation that inspires admiration, though
it comes from no less a thinker than Kant ; even agreeing that
holiness is the aim of life it is not necessary to conclude that
therefore endless progress is necessary in order to attain
this holiness or perfect accordance of the will with the moral
law. Even then, endless progress and endless duration are
terms as meaningless as endless time. One cannot help
feeling that the immortality of the soul had to be proved
somehow and that it is not so much the discovery of an
investigating mind as a preconceived notion which the
intellect, willingly or unwillingly, had to support with
argument and proof. Thus there is not one of the many

philosophical and theological arguments for immortality which cannot be disproved with equal force and be opposed by an equally logical statement denying the first. One cannot help feeling about most of them that they are but eager attempts to prove that continued existence, for which man yearns with a desire that demands satisfaction.

In many ways it is strange that man should be so eager for an endless continuation of an existence which, for the majority of men, holds more of suffering and disappointment than of joy. It might well seem that the continuation of such a life ' for ever and for evermore ' would be far more terrible than its cessation. Even if we imagine an immortal life which is all joy and no suffering, which is full of the good things lacking in our present life, is it not even then an appalling prospect to think of such a life continued for ever and ever, without end ? Have those who demand immortality so insistently ever tried to picture what a thousand or a million years of these so-called joys of life would mean ?

It is but natural that the poor woman, who has to slave all her life to keep a husband and children clothed and fed, should think with longing of a heaven to come where she can ' do nothing for evermore.' But does she realize that after a few hours, to say nothing of a few million years, of this divine inactivity she would yearn for something to do even if it were only the mending of a pair of celestial socks ? The ability to find spiritual joy without activity and continual change denotes an advanced stage of evolution. For most of us a holiday is but a time of increased exertions and activities ; a heaven of eternal rest would be a horror from which we would devoutly pray to be delivered. Yet a heaven of activity would inevitably mean a repetition of the same activities over and over again which would be equally unsatisfactory. We speak so readily of endless life and ask for it, but it is only our inability to picture the endless life for which we ask which makes it possible that we should desire a thing which, if realized, would be a punishment more terrible than any pictured in Dante's *Inferno*.

Is it not rather that in our fear for the utter cessation of existence with the death of the physical body we crave a continued existence and, in our relief at not being extinguished altogether, do not worry ourselves unnecessarily about our possible feelings a few million years hence ; our main concern is that the immediate fear has been allayed. It is not only in the affairs of our mortal life that we are ever willing to put off our difficulties of to-day by a loan or mortgage which will tide us over for a few years to come, and which will delay the day of reckoning. It always satisfies us to delay that day ; as long as we can succeed in shifting it back again and again we are not much troubled by the fact that, when the fatal day finally does come, it will be far worse than our present predicament. Do not the mediaeval stories of men who sold their souls to the devil for a few more years of life (and what devil would drive such unprofitable barter ?) show the same eagerness to defer the day of reckoning and to enjoy the present moment ?

In our fear of death we are but too willing to accept anything in a remote future as long as we can overcome the immediate terror of an end to existence.

THE DENIAL OF IMMORTALITY BY MATERIALISM

There is then much of lofty aspiration, but also much of craven fear in the demand for immortality, for an endless life. It is not only for the benefit of humanity that we desire our personality to survive, but for our own satisfaction : we fear extinction. And more than that, in our attitude in the present life it is in many cases the fear of the unknown hereafter with its alternatives of dread pains or celestial joys, which makes us try to do good and to abstain from evil. Without the sword of this uncertainty suspended over their heads, many might well indulge in things which now they fear to do, since punishment may follow. It is not a noble conception of life that inspired these words of Luther : ' If you believe in no future life I would not give a mushroom for your God. Do, then, as you like ! For if no God, then no devil, no hell, as with a fallen tree all is over when you die. Then plunge into lechery, rascality, robbery, murder ! ' Surely if the fear of hell or of punishment in some form is the only reason why we should abstain from evil our morality is worth but little. Infinitely nobler is the story, which Tsanoff relates in *The Problem of Immortality*, of a Saracen woman who walked down the streets of Damascus with a pan of fire in one hand and a jug of water in the other. ' What are you about to do ? ' a monk asked her, ' Burn up Paradise and put out the fires of hell so that man may do good for the love of God.' The soul of Luther might well ponder this story in his celestial home.

In many ways our attitude towards death is the measure of our spirituality. Did not John Ruskin once suggest that the truest test of anyone's character would be his behaviour if he knew, beyond the shadow of a doubt, that he had only a few months to live. If any of us had this inevitable prospect how would we live in the meantime ? Would we make a futile, final attempt to extract as much pleasure and enjoyment out of life as our remaining days would allow ? Would we spend the remainder of our lives trying to do good to others for sheer love of humanity ? Or would we spend our time in incessant prayer, imploring God to have mercy on our souls and to treat us better than we have treated Him ? It would indeed be a true test of our inmost aspirations, of our fears and hopes as well as of our beliefs and knowledge, if we had this choice to make.

It cannot be denied that there is more true nobility in many a convinced materialist, who, never doubting his entire cessation at the death of the body, yet lives an unselfish, self-sacrificing life, than there is in the devout believer whose morality needs the fears of hell and the promise of heaven.   There is a moral grandeur about a materialist philosopher like Epicurus, lacking in many an idealist.   Though the term ' Epicurean ' has come to mean a refined indulgence in the pleasures of the senses, Epicurus himself was far above such a sensual materialism.   Both in his own life and writings as in those of his disciple Lucretius there is a sublime impersonality, almost reminiscent of Buddhism in its joyful acceptance of the extinction of personality.   Does not Lucretius speak of his teacher as one who ' rescued life from such great billows and such thick darkness and moored it in so perfect a calm and so brilliant a light ? '   However mistaken the philosophical materialist may be in his conviction that our life ends with the death of the body, there is far more true worth in his impersonal dedication to human progress than there is in him who ever clamours for immortality, who desires reward and fears punishment.

The same impersonal nobility distinguishes the positivist philosophy ; a Comte would dedicate his life to the service of humanity in the firm belief that he would cease to be at death and that only his thoughts and actions would live on in the humanity he loved.   And the words of a Charles Bradlaugh, who could say that it was enough for him if his life served but as a bridge across which humanity could march onwards to a better and happier future, surely showed a far nobler and more unselfish philosophy of life than the above mentioned outburst of Luther, characteristic of a morality rooted in fear of punishment and hope of reward. However mistaken may be his conviction that our life ends with the death of the body, yet the materialist, who willingly faces such a complete extinction and yet works for the well-being of humanity, giving of his best to the last, is far superior in attitude and aims than the grovelling seeker after immortality, who, in pitiful concern for his own future is unable to give freely without bargaining with God for a return.

It is in the fear of death that Christianity has strayed sadly from the message of Christ. Surely, if ever a teacher proved in his life that man is more than his body and that the spirit can be triumphant even though materially the man may be conquered, it was the Founder of Christianity. It would almost seem as if He emphasized His teaching by coming among men without advantages of wealth, position, power or rank, surrendering all weapons and suffering Himself to be taken and killed by His enemies, that He might all the more abundantly prove the triumphant power of the spirit which lived and gained a world for Christianity. And yet there is no religion which nurses such a dismal fear of death than the Christianity which man made out of the teachings of the Gallilean. Is not a Christian funeral in its melancholy gloom the very denial of Christ's message, is not a Christian cemetery with the inscriptions upon its tombstones, telling us that ' here rests ' the one we knew in life, but a monument of unchristian beliefs ? Is it not incredible that one should hear Christians discussing the place where they will lie after death, choosing a beautiful spot as if they themselves were to lie under six feet of earth, sitting bold upright from time to time to take a look at the landscape ? Is it not here also time that we made our choice, either deciding to become Christians, accepting the message of the Master and putting far from us the materialistic gloom and pious lies on tombstones, or else frankly declaring that we hold Christ to have been a deluded one and that the body is all we are. There is no worse indictment of modern Christianity than the superstitious fear with which we surround the mystery of death, the hushed anxiety with which we speak of the one fact which is a certainty in the future of each one of us.

We can learn at least in this respect from those of other religions whom we are pleased to call heathens, but who in their attitude towards death are truer disciples of Christ than many Christians. See how the Hindu scheme of life, ordained thousands of years before our era, always had death in mind as the inevitable fact. The life of the Hindu of the higher castes is divided into four stages, those of the disciple, being prepared for life, the householder, doing his duty by the community in which he lives, the dweller in the forest who frees himself from the ties that bound him, surrendering possession and power and living the hermit life, and finally the wandering mendicant who has surrendered even the hermitage and is without a home, having renounced all that is of this world. It is true, but little remains of this organization of Hindu life, but even so death to the Hindu is a present reality in life and not a horrible phantom to be feared and, if possible, ignored. Instead of waiting for death to take from us, as we are pleased to express it, all that we hold dear and precious, the Hindu himself makes the surrender and, when death comes, man is ready and willing. However much modern India may have strayed from the laws of Manu even so Christian nations have still much to learn from the Orient which, in its implicit belief, nay, its certainty that the spirit lives even though the body dies, stands nearer to the teachings

of Christ than our Christian civilization with its abject fear
of death and its trembling hope of immortality. They might
well ponder the words of the Bhagavad Gita :

> Never the spirit was born, the spirit shall cease to be never ;
> Never was time it was not, end and beginning are dreams !
> Birthless and deathless and changeless remaineth the spirit
>   for ever ;
> Death hath not touched it at all, dead though the house
>   of it seems.

Modern Christianity is burdened by a materialism which is
a direct contradiction of its central teaching, a materialism
which lacks the nobility of the philosophical materialist,
being fraught with fear and concern for our personal fate.

THE RELATION BETWEEN BODY AND SOUL

The materialist looks upon the soul or consciousness as a
temporary by-product of the body and its functions, ceasing
with the death of that body ; consequently immortality has
no place in his philosophy. Yet it does not require much
introspection to discover that we cannot be the body or a
result of its functions. The very fact that we can restrain
and control the body, override its desires and tendencies,
make it do what it does not want to do, work when it wants
to rest, go without food when it wants to eat, drive it on
pitilessly when it wants to surrender and in supreme sacrifice
even give its life to save another's, shows that we are not
the body, much less a by-product of it, but rather the
power that moves it from within. Were we the body such
a thing as self-restraint or self-control, moral struggle or
self-sacrifice would be a philosophical impossibility. We
can only control that which we are not ; ' not-self control '
would be a more appropriate term than ' self-control,' which
does but express our identification with the body through
which we work.

This does not mean that we are not dependent on the body for our harmonious expression in the physical world ; should it become incapable of expressing our nature or be damaged in its functioning our own manifestation through it will be inhibited to that extent. We may well look upon the defective human being, such as the congenital idiot, as one whose bodily instrument is so damaged as to prevent the normal expression of the individual behind. When we alter the functions of the body, as for instance by the extraction or implantation of glands the possibilities of expression through the body will be changed so profoundly that we seem to be confronted by a human being different from the one we knew before. But to conclude from this that, consequently, the living individual is but a by-product of the body and to exclaim with a triumphant and unholy joy that now, at last, we have proved that the body is primary and man in his aspirations and creative effort is but secondary, is as unthinking and unfounded as it would be to say that the artist is but a by-product of his violin since, when a string is missing, the possibilities of his artistic expression are changed forthwith.

Yet we must not ignore the importance of the bodily instrument and its perfect functioning in the production of the soul's music. It is strange that, even though most of us unthinkingly identify ourselves with the bodies that are our instruments, we yet lack the good sense to take such care of these instruments that they will be capable of expressing us to the full.

Realizing, then, that we are not the body we use, but the living individual behind that body we must try to understand in what relation we stand to the body we use in the process of our evolution. In the chapter on ' Spirit and Matter ' we have seen that there is no fundamental duality in the universe, but that, according to our place in the scale of eternal creation, a thing appears to us as matter or as spirit, as life or as form. Thus our body appears as matter to us; yet in the light of Reality it is not fundamentally different from that which we are ourselves, but it belongs to a group of manifestations at a lesser level than we ourselves are.

We gain self-realization through our contact with these lesser manifestations, with which we subsequently identify ourselves. That identification is incarnation, the association of man with a lesser and to him material mode of being, which will afford him the limitation and separateness necessary for the fulfilment of his cycle of evolution.

In the earlier stage of his evolution man is entirely identified with the body and in that identification is but part of nature, this being the level of manifestation to which the body belongs. As a vague memory of his true being begins to stir within man there arises the awareness of duality, life within and body without, there begins moral struggle with its failures and triumphs, there begins conscious effort and aspiration, which finally lead to reality. When that is attained man knows that he and his body are one indeed in essence, but that the body is a lesser manifestation of eternal Reality, to be controlled and guided by him who uses it in the process of his evolution.

We therefore, are not our body, it is the instrument we use, through which we learn, through which we express ourselves. Neither are we essentially different from this body, it too is part of eternal Reality, though a lesser manifestation than we are. Since we are not our body our continued existence does not depend on the life of this body or cease at its death. This is not a proof of the immortality of the soul; it does but show that the life of the soul is not dependent on the life of the physical body, even though for its manifestation in this physical world, such a body is necessary to it.

SURVIVAL NOT IMMORTALITY

Continued existence after death is not immortality. However fully spiritualistic phenomena may prove the survival of our personality after death this but shows that, when the physical body dies, we live on in the after-death world, where we assimilate the experiences of the life through which we have just passed.

There is thus no improbability or impossibility whatsoever about the communion with those whom we are wont to call the dead. They are, of course, no more dead than we are, in fact, they can only be more alive, being temporarily freed of the limitation which identification with the physical body brings. This does not mean that the spirit announcing himself to an awed audience as Julius Caesar or Napoleon, uttering platitudes which even a mediocre mind would disdain, is necessarily the one he claims to be. There are many influences at work at a genuine spiritualistic séance, from the subconscious and dramatizing minds of those present, vagrant thoughts and ideas and possible non-human entities, to the occasional manifestation of a human individual who has gone through the change we call death. Even when the words spoken at a spiritualistic séance come from one who has passed into the next world, there is no reason to receive them with a mysterious awe as if they contained great wisdom ; the person who has passed into the next world is not necessarily any wiser than he was when he departed from this world ; his words do but prove that man survives the death of the body.

Important though this fact is, *it is no argument for the immortality of the soul*. Even the fact that we live through many hundreds of lives in the completing of our cycle of evolution does not imply immortality; since the end is return to the unity whence we came we may even say that there must necessarily be an end to our life as an individual since there was a beginning. Philosophically it does not matter whether our span of life is sixty years or, in our greater evolution, sixty million years; since an end must come we cannot speak of immortality.

The facts of spiritualism and the doctrine of reincarnation, however, change our attitude in so far, that we come to look upon death as but a normal change in our greater life, a change through which we, as individuals, have passed many a time and through which we shall pass many a time to come. Thus there is nothing to be feared in death, neither can we speak of those who have passed over as being in any way less alive than we are. In fact, we might well remember Shelley's lines :

> Peace, Peace ! he is not dead, he doth not sleep—
> He hath awakened from the dream of life—
> 'Tis we, who, lost in stormy visions, keep
> With phantoms an unprofitable strife,
> And in mad trance strike with our spirit's knife
> Invulnerable nothings. . . . .

We must then change our attitude with regard to the mystery of death and eliminate from our Christian civilization the dismal gloom with which, in such unchristian manner we surround the death of the body. In bringing about that change of attitude the fact of the survival of the individual beyond the death of the body, and the understanding of our life as but part of an age-long evolution, have indeed a profound value. But they do not prove immortality; the end of the individual's life is but postponed.

THE ILLUSION OF IMMORTALITY

Is immortality then philosophically possible ; are we not again in the throes of a wrong question which no ingenuity can ever solve ? Let us analyze how the question originates and see what elements enter into its nature.

To some extent we all identify ourselves with the bodies through which we are manifest in this particular life ; when we think of ourselves we imagine our physical appearance, associating with it our thoughts and feelings ; that to us is our real self. We think of ourselves with the name we bear and the face we have, the virtues and the shortcomings that are ours, and it is for that self that we ask immortality. It is true, we expect that in some miraculous way our vices and infirmities will fall away from us when once we enter the heavenly realm, and that all our virtues and excellencies will be enhanced, so that we shall indeed be glorified editions of what we are in this earthly life. Yet it is this earthly personality for which we claim endless existence, immortality ; when we think of ourselves as living on for ever and ever in the heaven world or in the infernal regions, we think of ourselves as the personalities that are ours now, with the appearance we have here. The claim for immortality, therefore, is made for the personality we feel ourselves to be in this life.

Furthermore we ask our question in the conception of time as an endless succession of events. *Only in the idea of time as an objective reality, continuing for ever and ever, can we think of immortality*. Immortality implies endless life, endless life implies endless time and endless time is a philosophical absurdity.

Time is not the objective reality we hold it to be in the illusion of our externalized world-image ; time is but our realization of eternity. The illusion of a time which either begins and ends, or else is endless, is but an outcome of our illusion of time as an absolute, objective reality. From that illusion is born our problem of immortality; when we overcome that illusion our problem is overcome also.

The other element in our quest of immortality is our illusion of being this temporary personality through which we are manifesting. If one were to ask, ' do you believe in the immortality of the soul ? ' it would be quite impossible to answer that question with ' yes ' or ' no.' We should first have to ask ' what do you mean by the soul ; do you mean yourself as you appear and exist now, with the characteristics associated with the personality that bears your name ? If so the answer is no ; that personality is of one life only and will cease to be, just as the many personalities through which we have expressed ourselves in past lives have ceased to be. If, therefore, you identify yourself with that personality you must cease to be with it. If, on the other hand, by the word ' soul ' you mean the reincarnating individual, the true Ego, who lives through many hundreds of lives on earth, then the answer is that in this individuality you will certainly survive the death of the body as you have survived the death of many bodies in the past and will survive the death of many more in the future. In so far, therefore, as you identify yourself with that more permanent self, the death of your present body and the dissolution of your present personality will matter but little ; you will live through all that. But even that is not immortality, that Ego too must cease to be. The Ego was born at individualization, and will cease to be when the creative Rhythm has been perfected, and we reach the at-onement in which we become all that is. Thus even the reincarnating self is not immortal ; though its life may stretch through many hundreds of thousands, if not millions,

of years there must come an end to it also. If, finally, by soul
you mean your eternal being, which unchangingly abides,
then again we cannot say that there is ' immortality ' for this
being. We here enter the world of Reality, where the terms
and structures of our world-image no longer apply.

ETERNAL REALITY

If we would experience truth we must disengage ourselves
from the illusions that bind us and enter the world of Reality.
When, in its light, we view the problem of immortality it
loses all meaning and importance, since in the world of the
Real the illusions, from which the problem was born, no
longer exist. Here we no longer experience time as one thing
after another ; in this world of Reality we experience
Eternity, in which all time is unchangingly contained.

In the eternal, past and future are a present reality, and
we are that reality. How, then, can we demand immortality
when we are eternal ? In our real being we are a reality
which has never begun and which will never end, a reality
which is unchanging. The idea of immortality is but a
distortion, in the illusion of our world-image, of that eternity
which we experience in the world of the Real ; it is but a
misinterpretation of that supreme Reality in the terms of an
objective-time illusion. How can we be concerned about
our future after death, when we know ourselves as the Eternal
which is future and past in abiding reality ? In the Eternal
we know that we cannot cease to be, because we are ; an end
is as impossible in the Eternal as would be a beginning, and
the demand for an endless life is but a contradiction in itself.

How futile and unworthy seems this demand for immortality, with its attendant hosts of arguments and proofs,
when once we have experienced ourselves as the Eternal and,

in that experience, have gained a certainty which disdains argument and needs no proof. Truly the experience of our own eternity leaves us with nothing more to fear and nothing more to hope; what place is there for hope or fear when we have certainty? There is no possibility of trembling anxiety, of hope for the best or fear for the worst, when we know ourselves as the Eternal, past and future, in unchanging reality. Yet it is not *we* who are that reality, what we call 'ourselves' in the illusion of our world-image is but our changing experience of eternal Reality.

Our eternal being is not a far-off hope, not an uncertain heaven which may become our part; we are the Eternal now, at this moment, as at all moments of what we call 'time.' We always seek in the wrong direction, we always want *more* time; we demand even endless time in our quest of immortality. Yet the infinitely greater Reality is ever ours to enter if we but will, whereas the lesser claim is but an illusion, born of illusion. We do not want more time, we want eternity in which all time is; we need to strike out in a different dimension altogether. Instead of wanting ever more and more of our time-experience we should, at this very moment, pierce through the veil of time and enter eternity, which can be found in fullness at every moment of our time. Instead of yearning to go on to the next moment, the next experience in time, we should go *into* the moment, *into* the present, and here and now enter eternity. The depth of the Eternal is in every instant of time, and we shall find it if we will but abandon illusion and enter reality. We need not wait for some glory to come, the Glory is here, now, if we will but realize it. How unworthy seems the demand for immortality when we experience eternity!

In that experience we are no longer the separate self, we are no longer what we call 'we' in our daily life. Not only are we our entire being, past and future, in that sublime experience of eternity, but we are the reality of all that is, was, or shall be, we are *That*. Knowing this, the demand for immortality of the separate and passing self appears even more vain ; it is almost blasphemy that the shifting phase of a creature in the illusion of its world-image should demand for itself an endless continuation of its illusory experience. When we read of man's fear and trembling in his search for immortality, of his petty concern for his own small self, of the meaningless arguments and proofs which, through the ages, he has called in to defend the phantasm which he dare not think untrue, it is with a feeling of liberation that we shake off this complicated ingenuity with which man constructed his castle of errors and enter the pure air of the world of Reality. There, in the world of the Real, in a divine simplicity, we experience ourselves as that Eternity, in the light of which all fears and hopes become superfluous. We are freed from the entanglements of illusion with its problems and from our vain attempts to solve them. We no longer seek immortality ; we know the Eternal.

CHAPTER ELEVEN

IN THE LIGHT OF THE ETERNAL

He that knows what truth is, knows what that light is ; and he that knows it, knows eternity. Charity knows it. O eternal truth ! and true Charity ! and dear Eternity ! Thou art my God, to Thee do I sigh day and night.—ST. AUGUSTINE.

THE MEANING OF LIFE

WE have then fulfilled our quest of Reality ; our voyage of exploration is done. It is true we have seen but a little of that world of Reality which is wide and great as eternity, in which is all that ever was or can be. Yet our discoveries are more than a reward for the hardships we undergo when we leave that which is familiar for that which is unknown. We indeed did leave the world we knew so well and set out on a perilous quest for reality and living truth. And see, in the new world where we arrived, we found our old world back, but in its true and everlasting meaning, knowing which our old world can never be the same again. We have ascended the mountain of Reality and from its top we have seen the vision of things as they are. With that vision in our hearts we can safely descend and return to the valleys where men live, for wherever we go the vision of the mountain-top will be before our eyes and we shall see all things, even the most familiar, in the light of the Eternal. We have heard the song of eternal Creation and in that song even the harsher sounds of this world of illusions have gained a profound and lasting meaning, what to us appeared as suffering and evil is seen to be as much and as necessarily part of that eternal song as that which to us appears as joy and righteousness. Having seen the vision, having heard the song, we can live indeed.

But do not all men live, do we not share their life as they share ours ? Truly, we have in common the life of the body, we eat and drink and rest and work, we provide that which is necessary to keep our body alive and in health, but that alone is not the fullness of life for man. Unless there is meaning and purpose in the life we live, unless we know why we suffer and rejoice, why we toil and exert ourselves why we live in this physical body, why first it rules us and then we learn to rule it, unless we can see all that in the light of Reality we do not truly live, we but exist.

Is it not strange how so many can live without knowing, without asking why ? If we were to ask any one of these to undertake a task involving many hardships and yet did not tell him why, did not show sufficient reason to warrant the undertaking of the task, would he do it ? Would any one of us undertake even a journey of a few hundred miles without knowing why, without having some purpose ? And yet, so many of us live, undertaking not a chance task, but the great Task of life itself, going, not some chance journey, but the great Journey of Life itself, with hardships and sufferings greater than any mortal journey may bring, and yet we ask not why. If we can look upon our human life as from a mountain top it seems but a delusion of insanity in which the millions hurry to and fro, apply themselves to their daily tasks, live in worry and anxiety, or hope in joyful expectations, despair when they fail or exult in success, not knowing the meaning of their lives. When we go through the streets of some great city and watch the faces of the men and women whom we meet, full of concern, of worry and discontent, of unhappiness and even of anger and hatred, we may well wonder whence all this grim solemnity if they neither know nor ask the purpose of life itself ? What an empty show of activity is our hurry and bustle, our rushing to and fro in activities, upon which we look as of the utmost importance, if there is no definite meaning in all this tremendous expenditure of energy !

And looking from the faces of our fellowmen to the shops in which are displayed the products of their activity, the majority ugly and tawdry, a still greater majority useless and only a few beautiful and necessary in life, do we not stand amazed at the blind ignorance which can load down our lives with the burden of such superfluous ugliness ? Truly certain things are necessary in life. We must have food and drink so that our bodies may live, healthy and clean food, refreshing and wholesome drink, we must have clothing to protect ourselves against heat and cold, we must have homes in which our lives may be centred, where we can find a haven of rest and a serene happiness. We need machinery, the technical perfection of our outer life, by means of which we can transcend our surroundings and control our material life. We need art and science, philosophy and religion, we need all that will make life deeper and more joyful, richer and fuller. But we do not need food which is but harmful and productive of disease, we do not want dress which is ugly and a mistaken gratification of vanity, we do not want homes which are so elaborate that they become centres of disturbance instead of harmony and rest, we do not want machinery and mechanical contrivances which destroy life instead of furthering it, which enslave humanity instead of setting it free. We do not want science that causes suffering nor art which is untrue and vulgar, we need no philosophy which is but a play of words, nor a religion in which a

man-made God is served with man-made dogmas, obscuring
the eternal message of living truth, which the great Teachers
of all ages have brought to man. We need far less and at
the same time far more, above all we need the understanding
which will show us what is necessary and life-giving and
what is superfluous and destructive.

When we realize the eternal meaning of life we can see
how much there is in life that is superfluous and even
harmful, we can see how much there is that can be spared
and must be eliminated, but at the same time we can see how
much is lacking, how much *more* we need. The simplicity
of real life can truly manage with but a fraction of the
manifold encumbrances and complexities of modern life,
but at the same time it demands a far higher standard of
beauty and utility in those things which are essential. Truly
we cannot arrange our lives wisely unless we know the
meaning of life ; we shall but continue to seek our riches
where no riches are, to waste our energies where they do but
harm, forgetting all the while the wisdom of Ruskin's saying :
' There is no wealth but life.'

Only when we have seen life as from a mountain top do
we know true values, true greatness. As long as we err in
the valley of illusion we judge but by the illusory externals
which loom so large in our sight, we see appearance, not
reality. Does not our judgment of man bear witness to our
worship of externals ; would not most of us, if placed by
magic in the time when Christ lived, look upon the Roman
rulers of His age as men great and worthy, successful and
important, would we not yearn for their approval and take
in their every word ? And would most of us not look with
contempt upon the Man of Nazareth, poor and powerless,
belonging to a despised race, daring to set himself up as an
authority above the mighty ones of His day ? Would we give

Him the same attentive ear which we would give to those great in the public eye, with power over life and death, would we have been capable to see that He alone was worth listening to, that He alone was great and wise and powerful, and that in the light of His eternal greatness the impressive pomp and seeming power of even the greatest of Romans were but as nothing ? Indeed, even after ages of Christianity, our judgment of values is but an unchristian one, we judge by the tinsel of outer appearance, and are blind and deaf to the wonders of reality within. We know not the meaning of things.

PRACTICAL PHILOSOPHY

That meaning philosophy can reveal to us. Philosophy is, or at least should be, the most practical activity of man. It is true, but too often has philosophy been a play of abstract ideas, of profound interest in its subtle shades of meaning to the professional philosopher, but without practical meaning to the man in the street in his daily life. It is conceivable, therefore, that the average man has wondered at times how there could be those who would, as it seems to him, waste their time in abstract speculation while there was so much to do in practical life for the helping of mankind. And yet, if philosophy is what it should be, realization of life, it cannot fail to be of the most vital importance and interest to man in his daily life. It brings the experience of the meaning of life, and in that experience alone can we learn what is worth while in our activities, what of real value in our achievements.

If we rush into activity, without having this realization of philosophy, we are as a man who undertakes a long journey without first acquainting himself with the nature of the country through which he must travel and the road he must follow. If we were to offer such a man the help of our experience by explaining to him a map of the country through which he has to find his way, and if he disdained such help, saying that it was not practical, that only in *doing* the thing, practical reality could be found, we should surely look upon such an one as foolish. In a similar way, if a man were to voyage across the ocean and disdained to learn the principles of navigation and the use of the compass, saying that all such theory was but superfluous and unpractical and that the right thing to do was to set out and undertake the voyage, we should again consider such an one as unpractical and lacking in wisdom. Yet in our daily lives we do disdain the knowledge of the country through which we must all travel, we do disdain the map which philosophy can show us and we have no time to learn the navigation of life and the use of its compass which the experience of Reality alone can teach. How can we act unless we know what is worth achieving ? How can we choose unless we know real values ? How can we steer our ship across the ocean of life if we do not know whither we are bound and how to find our way ?

Philosophy is of the uttermost practical value in the life of everyday ; we cannot truly govern our lives without its help. Still less can we govern the life of nations ; politics, without philosophy to inspire and to direct, are but a dangerous play with the fate of nations and not a conscious direction of their evolution. In another volume we shall see how the realization of the creative Rhythm, which philosophy brings, yields that knowledge of historical evolution which enables the philosopher-statesman to legislate for his country in accordance with its evolution instead of deciding his political measures by the clash and strife of the selfish interests of groups within the nation. Could anything be more unpractical than the unscientific government of nations which has landed the world to-day in its chaotic difficulties ?

Could there be more damning evidence for the lack of true philosophy in our politics than the catastrophes which have overtaken humanity of late ? It is but ignorance of the forces at work in social life, national as well as international, and ignorance of the way to control them that causes these sufferings to mankind. A science of government, based not on a philosophy of abstract speculation, but on a philosophy of experience, would surely be infinitely more practical and more beneficial than the present unscientific government in which the blind do but lead the blind.

It is not enough to say that philosophy has practical value, we must acknowledge that the control of life, for the individual as well as for the nation, *is impossible* without the light of philosophical knowledge, as impossible as navigation without map or compass, as impossible as travelling without even knowing the direction in which the goal of our travels is to be found. Our very behaviour depends on our philosophy.

WORLD-AFFIRMATION AND WORLD-DENIAL

Our practical behaviour in life is always the outcome of our attitude towards the world surrounding us, whether we are conscious of it or not. If we look upon this world as objective reality we shall seek our happiness in it, if on the other hand we see it as illusion or as evil, we shall fly from this world in our search for happiness. It is here that the experience of Reality alone can deliver us from the problem by which we find ourselves confronted as long as we do not know the measure of reality of this world of ours.

There is a period in the evolution of man when he is wholly identified with that world, when he is but part of nature and lives its life, following the impulses and desires of his body like any other animal. Such a life may be beautiful and full of joy, as the life of an animal may well be, but it is a life in which man is entirely subject to the world of nature and does not know his own slavery, exulting in his bondage. This is the true Paganism, where man is natural man, one with nature since he has not yet learned to know himself.

There comes a time when this unconscious and dream-like unity is lost, when man, in the separateness of individualism, feels himself apart from the world that surrounds him, separate from his fellowmen. In that duality he becomes conscious of the bondage which he did not realize before, he will feel in himself the body with its desires and the mind with its aspirations. In the inevitable struggle which follows he will seek to learn the meaning of the world surrounding him and will either affirm it as supreme reality or else deny it as a snare and a delusion. If he affirms it in theory and in practice then in his practice of life he is but a natural man, rejoicing in a belated Paganism which can never bring lasting satisfaction, since ever again the voice of the spirit within will speak and assert its aspirations, its claims. On the other hand, he may deny the world surrounding him, proclaiming it to be illusion, or even the very abode of wickedness, the seat of evil. Thus we see the Indian yogi, dead to the world, living in utter renunciation, suppressing every claim of the body so that the spirit may live. Thus we see the Christian ascetic fleeing from the world of evil into the peace of the hermitage, chastizing the body, so that its desires and passions may be crushed out. In this denial of the world and all that is of the world, man seeks salvation by putting all that is worldly far from him, looking upon those who pursue worldly aims as lost in darkness and bound for destruction.

World-affirmation and world-denial may at this stage well seem the only two alternatives. If there is an objective world surrounding us from all sides we must either affirm it, recognizing its reality and its claims, or else deny it either as non-existing, as illusion, or as a snare and a wickedness, evil incarnate. It is true we may attempt a compromise— and what else is our conventional morality but such a compromise—in which we recognize the claims of the spirit within and of the world without and try to give each its due. The life of compromise, however, leads nowhere ; we dare not enjoy material life to the full, without regret ; we dare not reject that world and seek the spirit for fear that we may abandon happiness and riches for an uncertain bliss.

The aspirations of humanity have ever swayed to and fro between world-denial and world-affirmation ; even now the West is representative of the one and the East of the other. Does not our Western civilization glory in its physical power, in its dominion over this world ? Has it not asserted the reality of this world even to the exclusion of the world within, forgetting that man cannot live by bread alone ? And has not the East, in its assertion of spiritual reality within, rejected the world without, disdaining to gain power, knowledge and control of that world and thereby becoming, at least materially, a prey to the nations of the West ? It is true, both in East and West there have been those who have found Reality and whose mode of life has borne witness to their supreme experience. The Buddha taught the Middle Way which was neither world-denial nor world-affirmation, still less a compromise. Even so taught Christ, nor can He be held responsible for the misrepresentation of his message by disciples and followers who, lacking the experience of Reality, limited the message of their Teacher to the measure of their own minds. The extravagance of Christian asceticism is not the fruit of Christ's teaching, nor the self-seeking materialism which in so strange a manner claims for itself the sanction of the Christian Church. Still less did Christ teach a life of compromise, even though conventional morality too seeks its refuge in the teachings of Christianity.

On the whole, however, the West has affirmed the world, the East has denied it. The strength of the one is the weakness of the other; the West is as powerful in the noisy clamour of outer activity as the East is in the silent 'inactivity' of the spirit. The achievement of each seems but as emptiness in the eyes of the other; the East has a good-humoured smile for the illusory achievements of the West, just as the West has a hardly concealed contempt for the inactivity of the East. And yet there is value and meaning in each. We of the West do not always recognize the power of silence and of inactivity, our inactivity is but too often laziness; our silence ineptitude. But there is a silence more eloquent than the most impassioned oratory, there is an inactivity more powerful than the most frenzied action. Is it not the silent man, measured in his words and actions, who is often the strongest leader in a time of crisis? And do not our deepest emotions defy expression in words, are we not speechless in our greatest sorrow as well as in our greatest joy? We do not speak in the presence of death, neither do we speak when we meet the long lost friend after many years of sorrowful separation, and yet, our silence is infinitely more expressive than words could possibly be. There is power to be gained in world-denial as well as through world-affirmation, but which are we to choose?

The problem surely is not one foreign to daily life, it is the very foundation of our behaviour, the basis of our morality. Are we to recognize this world surrounding us alone as real? Then let us plunge into its activities, enjoy to the full its pleasures, not pausing to consider, never stopping to think. Let us then seek achievement and power in that world, let us try to be great there, amass its riches, grasp its pleasures. If on the other hand that world is not real, or, worse even, if it is the power that eternally opposes us, the power of evil, then let us put far from us this world and its temptations, let us forsake it, renouncing the pleasures it holds out and seek the solitude within, the spirituality which there we can find.

Truly, without the vision of the Real the problem is as difficult as it is momentous and yet there seems no alternative, either we must live the life of the world or else the life of spirituality, unless we consent to surrender to a life of compromise which is empty of meaning.

THE PRACTICE OF REALITY

Let us then once again analyze our problem and see whether or not it is capable of solution. We speak of world-affirmation and of world-denial. But what is that world which we seek either to affirm or to deny ? It is the world which we see around us, the world which appears as an objective reality, distinct from the life within. But that world is only an image in my consciousness ; it is but my interpretation of Reality. It is true, I externalize that world-image, believing it to be a reality outside my consciousness, but that does not make it the reality it appears to be. Neither can I say that it is all illusion, that it does not exist at all and that, therefore, it should be ignored and rejected in the practice of daily life. We cannot say of the externalized world-image either that it is real or that it is unreal ; it is both real and unreal. It is real in so far as it is our interpretation of Reality, it is unreal in so far as it is not Reality itself, but only our interpretation. The illusory part of it is that we dissociate from our consciousness that which is only image in it and proclaim it to be independent reality.

To deny that externalized world-image is as impossible as to affirm it ; in denying it we deny the fact that in our consciousness the world of Reality produces an image which we externalize and call ' the world.' To affirm that world as reality is equally impossible ; at its best it is but our interpretation or image of reality, never the objectively real world which we believe it to be.

Our universe then is no objectively real world which we can either affirm or deny. The whole problem of world-denial and world-affirmation is but born of the illusion in which we place outside of our consciousness as objective reality that which is but image in it, caused by eternal Reality. Our problem is once again born of illusion and incapable of solution. We cannot affirm our objectivated world-image as reality, we cannot deny it as illusion, still less as evil and wicked. We can only try to understand it as it really is and treat it accordingly.

In the experience of reality we know things as they are, since we are all that is. That real world, the reality of things, can neither be affirmed nor denied ; we are that supreme Reality ourselves, sharing the eternal being of all things. When from the experience of Reality we return to the dream of our world-image we no longer identify ourselves with it, thinking it to be the only reality, neither do we shrink from it as from a world of evil, or ignore it as a mere glamour of illusion. We can now see it all the time as that which it is—the image produced in our consciousness by eternal Reality, our interpretation of things as they are. Such an attitude is neither world-denial nor world-affirmation, it is *the contemplation of our world-image in the light of the Eternal*. The great change brought about by our

experience of Reality is that we can now see our world-image
as interpretation of Reality ; we can see the appearances
of daily life as phases or moments of that eternal Reality
which we know within.

In the light of that Reality the passing appearance gains a
new meaning, a new dignity, which without the vision of the
Real it could not have. Round us we see all the time forms
that are changing, nothing abides, all is in a process of
eternal becoming. These ever-changing phases are but
meaningless if seen by themselves, they become full of a
wonderful meaning when seen as our realization of eternal
Reality. This is a revelation of Reality, affecting life so
deeply that no words can describe its meaning to one who
has not seen his world in the light of the Eternal. What
takes place is truly a transmutation of our world, without any
change in that world itself, but merely by virtue of the fact
that we can now all the time *see our world-image as interpretation of eternal Reality*. It is perhaps the greatest gift of the
philosophy of experience that all things in their time illusion,
events in life as well as problems of life, are now seen in the
light of the Eternal.

When we have seen the vision of Reality our world is
changed, utterly and almost beyond recognition, and yet
nothing has changed in things as they are, it is but that *we*
have gained a new vision. Ugliness and suffering, dishar-
mony and evil only exist for us as long as we see our world-
image as an objective reality, as long as we see things by
themselves. The moment we can see the objects and events
of our world as the interpretation by us of Reality, the eternal
meaning of the thing in itself is revealed through its appearance in our world ; we see the changing object, the passing
event in the light of the Eternal. In that light they can no
longer be ugly or evil ; they all share the grandeur of eternal

Reality. Does not Shelley describe in the *Prometheus Unbound* how, with the fall of Jupiter, King of Illusion, the whole world is changed ?

> . . . and soon
> Those ugly human shapes and visages
> Of which I spoke as having wrought me pain,
> Past floating through the air, and fading still
> Into the winds that scattered them ; and those
> From whom they past seemed mild and lovely forms
> After some foul disguise had fallen, and all
> Were somewhat changed, and after brief surprise
> And greetings of delighted wonder, all
> Went to their sleep again ; and when the dawn
> Came, wouldst thou think that toads, and snakes, and efts,
> Could e'er be beautiful ? yet so they were,
> And that with little change of shape or hue ;
> All things had put their evil nature off. . . .

It is in the new vision, which is born when man is freed from the tyranny of illusion, that the whole world is changed and appears radiant with love and beauty, apparently utterly changed, though the change really is in man himself alone. When we can see the world around us, our world-image, in the light of Reality every detail of it is suffused by the light of the Eternal and in that light gains a new beauty and a profound meaning. It is *in ourselves that the key to our world-image is to be found ;* with our fuller realization that image changes until it is truly seen as ' the shadow of Beauty unbeheld.' In the deep realization of the poet, which was Shelley's, he expresses the liberation of man from the bonds of his self-created illusions in words which no philosophical expression of truth can attain :

> The painted veil, by those who were, called life,
> Which mimicked, as with colours idly spread,
> All men believed and hoped, is torn aside ;
> The loathsome mask has fallen, the man remains
> Sceptreless, free, uncircumscribed, but man
> Equal, unclassed, tribeless, and nationless,

Exempt from awe, worship, degree, the king
Over himself ; just, gentle, wise : but man
Passionless ? no, yet free from guilt or pain,
Which were, for his will made or suffered them,
Nor yet exempt, though ruling them like slaves,
From chance, and death, and mutability,
The clogs of that which else might oversoar
The loftiest star of unascended heaven,
Pinnacled dim in the intense inane.

' The man remains,' and in him is found the secret of Reality.

IN THE LIGHT OF THE ETERNAL

It is only while we still see our world-image as an objectively real world that its appearances can be to us objects
of desire and that we can pursue them, intent on possession.
Desire is but the expression of the belief in our world-image
as objective reality ; we pursue in a vain attempt at possession
those images which arise in our consciousness and inevitably
experience disillusion when we discover that they are but—
appearance. Equally vain is the repudiation of that world-
image, we cannot escape it, as little as we can desire it ; our
attempts at escape will but bind us all the closer to the world
from which we fly. To put from us the world, proclaiming
it to be full of illusion and wickedness is not true spirituality,
it is but the outcome of error and can only cause suffering to
those who make it their goal.

The spirituality born of the experience of Reality is very
different. In it we neither desire the appearances of our
world-image, nor do we reject or fear them ; we know them
for what they are, images produced in our consciousness,
and see them as our interpretation of the Eternal.

When we enter the world of Reality and become established
in it, desire becomes superfluous since we are all that is and
there is nothing to desire outside Reality. How can we want
a thing when we are all things, and experience all things as

our own being ? In the peace of the Eternal desire grows silent and that, which we never could possess while we pursued it in our world-image, is ours eternally, since we are that thing itself. The play of desire is but the play with our own world-image as externalized reality ; when we are That which produces the world-image such play becomes superfluous.

Our joy in the beauties of our world-image, the world we see surrounding us, will now be far greater than before, since in all that surrounds us we can see that deeper beauty, that greater joy—the Eternal shining through the veil of time. In real spirituality, therefore, we do not desire the forms of the world-image since we are one with the Reality that produces them, neither do we shrink from them since we see them in the light of their eternal meaning. We can thus live in the world and yet not be of the world ; we can do our work in the world to the best of our ability, concentrating our energies and our powers on it and yet be free from attachment to that which is but our experience of Reality. There is no need to seek holiness in poverty and solitude ; there is holiness wherever we find ourselves placed in our daily life, since everywhere is the Eternal.

Such is the sanctification of the world. We no longer need the seclusion of the church to find God and to serve Him, we see Divinity in the faces of our fellowmen, and hear its music in the voices of nature. Our daily life has become the cathedral in which we revere the Eternal, while the common activities of our human existence have become the ceremonial in which we worship the Reality which in them is manifest.

In the light of Reality there is no word or action that is not part of Eternity, since all are our realization of the Eternal. It is truly as if a Light from within now illumined our world-image ; every object in it, every creature has a profound and eternal message when seen in the light of the Eternal. The world of time has become the symbol of eternity ; in the light of the Eternal time itself is eternalized. It is only as long as we are bound in illusion that things can appear as meaningless, as wrong, as lost in chaos ; when we have seen Reality there is not a grain of dust which has not a sublime meaning, since it is for ever part of the Eternal.

We ourselves derive a new meaning from this Partnership ; we now may walk in time, but we live in the Eternal, we may behold illusion, but we know Reality. Such are the fruits of the Vision of the Eternal, such is the practice of Reality. To see Reality is to live ; to become It is to have achieved.

In that achievement alone is Peace and Liberation.